Additional Praise for River Jordan

"River Jordan writes with a hard-bitten confidence comparable to Ernest Hemingway. And yet, in the Southern tradition of William Faulkner, she knits together sentences that can take your breath."

—*Florida Today*

"River Jordan is the South's Anne Lamott: hilarious, authentic, irreverent, and breathtakingly insightful about all things spiritual."

—Joy Jordan-Lake, author of *A Tangled Mercy*

"Beautifully written, atmospheric."

—*Kirkus Reviews*

"Raw-boned. Unflinching. Gut-level honest."

—Bren McClain, author of *One Good Mama Bone*

"River Jordan's words flat-out sing. One may speed-read the paper, the grocery list, and the email, but not the words of River Jordan. Her stories court you to pace yourself and give them their due."

—Shellie Rushing Tomlinson, author of
*Suck Your Stomach In & Put Some Color On!:
What Southern Mamas Tell Their Daughters
that the Rest of Y'all Should Know Too*

THE ANCIENT WAY

THE
ANCIENT
WAY

Discoveries
on the Path
of Celtic
Christianity

RIVER JORDAN

Broadleaf Books

Minneapolis

THE ANCIENT WAY
Discoveries on the Path of Celtic Christianity

Cover design by Laura Drew
Illustration by RedKoala/shutterstock

Print ISBN: 978-1-5064-6045-1
eBook ISBN: 978-1-5064-6046-8

For Saint James of Glasgow, for Iona,
and all the stories in between.

contents

PART THREE   A SUNDAY KIND OF HOPE

PART FOUR   TIME IS A TRAVELER

PART FIVE   IONA ON THE HILL

This is what the LORD says:
> Stand by the roadways and look.
> Ask about the ancient paths:
> Which is the way to what is good?
> Then take it
> and find rest for yourselves.

—JEREMIAH 6:16

Out of Ireland they came, bearing Celtic names and breathing holy power.

—"THE CELTIC MISSIONARIES OF IRELAND"

PROLOGUE: THE CALL
OF THE BELLS

*O*NCE UPON A TIME *in a land far away, a little girl ran away with the Roma—or gypsies, as many called them. She was just six years old, and so was still true to her own nature—a wild and beautiful thing.*

Before she ran away, the girl lived with her father and mother, who had left the New Country to work in the Old Country, a few miles beyond the ancient, walled city of Amberg, Germany. The girl felt she'd been exiled from the holy land of her home on the shores of the swampy Gulf Coast of Florida. Without consent, she'd been ushered to a cold place away from her beloved grandmother and her playmates and cousins. Being an only child, she thought, as all only children do, I am all alone in this world. *She never felt this to be more true than during those first days when she had been taken so far from the faces she knew and loved. To her, the grey skies of the Old Country were interminable, summers were short, and sunshine, a rare and precious commodity.*

They lived in one of seven bland, six-story buildings on the edge of vacant fields, and beyond those was a dark forest. These were the old times, and the old ways still ran through the people and the land, and there remained room to roam.

One particular summer day, the girl was playing outside within the shadows of the buildings, which marked the children's boundary because it kept them within earshot of their mothers. With windows open, a mother inside could hear the gentle sounds of play, or the cry of a child in trouble, or, worse, if all suddenly turned to silence. Silence meant secrets, or rules being broken. The girl always obeyed the rule of the shadow. Until the day she didn't.

If you are ever lucky enough for Roma to come passing by you with their horses and wagons, you will hear—as the little girl did that day—the tinkling of their bells, strung this way and that, announcing their arrival long before they are seen. As the ground rocks beneath their feet, the bells sing out the song of their freedom.

We are free, and we are wild,
and tonight we will dance beneath the moon,
below a canopy of stars.
We shall laugh, and we shall drink, and we shall
*   sing.*
We are alive; we are alive; we are alive.

First among the children to hear the bells, the girl stopped playing and walked to the edge of the shadow, her eyes searching intently for the source of the hypnotic sound. Soon the other children turned too, to gaze across the stretch of field as the wagons rolled into view and then cut away toward the woods in the distance.

The girl stepped out into the light, cupping her hands to shelter her eyes from the sun for a better view. Without another thought or a dare or permission, she dropped her hands and ran full force, determined to catch the wagons. Timidly, a few other children followed, then all of them left in pursuit. This is when the silence of the shadows began.

A spark, an urgency, twinged through the girl's body. Soon she was far, far ahead of the other children. One by one they fell behind, until they had all stopped and returned to the safety of the shadow. As the children's shouts faded behind the girl, she realized she alone was nearing the caravan.

The sky was an ocean of blue, and the girl felt a completely new sense of elation coursing through her—something that had been absent thus far from her short, serious life. She reveled in this sense of emancipation. The sun was warm on the top of her head, and her hair flew out long and loose over her shoulders, bouncing as she flew. Her heart soared and her spirits lifted.

Then the girl heard her name called, over and over. She ran on as her mother's voice grew fainter and more frantic. But suddenly, the girl felt a weight on her heart, as if a rock had tumbled up from the ground and lodged in her chest. And as another rock, and another, tumbled up and piled on, she knew with a deep sadness that she had to return to the arms of her mother. She ran on, but her steps slowed, until finally she stopped and stood still, her mother's voice now a small flutter.

The girl stood motionless, alone in the field, watching the wagons until their sound became a mere echo of bells. Until their coming and going seemed but a dream. Then the girl, head hung low, turned. And in sad, plodding steps she walked back into the shadow that wasn't her life.

PART 1

TRUSTING THE WIND

Kublai asked Marco:
"You, who go about exploring
and who see signs,
can tell me toward which of these futures
the favoring winds are driving us."

—CALVINO

I want to seize fate by the throat.

—LUDWIG VAN BEETHOVEN

I shall never believe that God plays dice with the world.

—ALBERT EINSTEIN

1

SONGLINES AND SALTWATER COWBOYS

I WAS BORN A SALTWATER girl and raised in the swampy land that runs along the Gulf of Mexico. You can stand on the beach and hear the waves roll in and, with white sand beneath your feet, throw a rock to hit a brackish lake. Drive a few miles inland and the brackish turns to clear blue springs, creeks full of freshwater fish, and pine trees. It is a place filled with such wonders as honeysuckle vines, magnolia trees, and blackberries growing in patches that have gone to wild. Heat-lightning storms on August nights. Full-moon summers. The southern landscape an intoxication as the earth longs for your embrace.

Among those who understand the earth's reach for our embrace are indigenous peoples. In Australia the indigenous people have an ancient form of communication known as songlines. As someone who is not a part of that culture, I am hard pressed to completely understand and communicate what songlines are, and what they are not. In spite of this limitation, I offer my humble attempt.

Songlines are memorized and handed down from generation to generation as a way of connecting people to their ancestors and to the divine. Songlines tell stories, but they also show the way back and the way forward. Some songlines can be used as a literal map, as they tell the geography of a region. Some songlines are ancient, such as "The Tale of the Seven Sisters," an epic story of mystery and creation that weaves across the Australian landscape and reaches up into the skies.

Imagine an album by one of your favorite artists—say, *The White Album* by the Beatles, or Tina Turner's *Private Dancer*—as a detailed story that shows you how to drive the historic Route 66, describing how the landscape will change as you travel, what weather you can expect along the way, what types of plants you will discover, and which ones are edible or medicinal; the wildlife you will likely encounter, which ones you can eat, and which might try to eat you. As if that were not enough, imagine that it tells you about your ancestors who traveled Route 66 before you, recounting their lives, their stories, their bravery, and the lessons they learned along the way. It speaks to you of something called "dreamtime" and of how all things came to be.

Now imagine there is a song for every road in your village or city, your state or province, your country and continent. And that these songs have been handed down for generations, providing a library of oral history that encapsulates the entire life of a people, their history, their creation, the landscape of the earth and the skies that tie them to the Creator. In this way the songlines become a tapestry of the people and can be used to navigate the way forward to your destination, whether that is literally to travel from the mountains to the sea, or is the landscape of metaphor—to travel within yourself to search out your soul and discover what you might find in the spirit world.

Although songlines seem a world away from me in distance and culture, one day several years ago I began considering them. They spoke to me in ways I understood. They told stories that were integral to the land, to finding my way both by the power of story and by knowing well the dirt where I walk. The event I'm about to recount was the first of a set of coincidences that crisscrossed my path, related to Celtic Christianity. I began to follow, letting them lead me along like one of the songlines of Australia—or the bells of a passing caravan.

This particular March day, I was in Apalachicola, Florida, a place I had visited frequently since childhood, an hour from my hometown of Panama City. The beaches of the Gulf Coast take a natural curve just before Apalachicola, forming a bay. As a result, rather than white sand, one discovers a beach of shells, and waters with just the right mix of brine to make oyster beds spring to life and produce oysters fit for kings and gods. (All oyster eaters are in agreement on this.)

This is a place of fishermen, shrimpers, and oystermen who stride high and mighty on the land like saltwater cowboys. They are heroes with rough hands and red necks and creases about their eyes. Their hair is bleached to blonde, or sometimes white, by so many hours in the sun. They can look at the sky and smell the air and know if there will be calm seas or if a gale is brewing. Or if it will be a bad year for hurricanes. One shrimper looked out at the waves one afternoon long ago, then turned to me and said, "It's gonna be a bad one for the storms this year." He nodded at me, then looked back out to the horizon, up to the skies, squinting in spite of the clouds, and added, "It's the back side of a 'cane that'll kill you."

They are connected to the land this way; they feel its rhythms and its breathing. Saltwater isn't something they simply use to catch their count and haul it ashore. Saltwater runs in their veins; the Gulf of Mexico is their sister, for which they are exceedingly thankful. And there is always plenty of time. That's what land like this tells you. *No need to hurry. We've got all the time we need right here in our pocket.*

Over the years, tourists wandered up this way, as did retirees craving the quiet, sleepy cove of Apalachicola (or "Apalach," to locals). Here, progress had paused. It was like stepping through a portal of time. Things remained unchanged. Until they didn't.

Small stores sprang up, little cottages, tiny coffee shops. The kind of quaint, local businesses that catered to visitors.

Still, the fishermen, the shrimpers, the oystermen walked the streets, sat at the bars, not quite irritated with this new tide of locals and day-trippers. Not just yet, anyway. To them it was still a workingman's paradise.

One anomaly of the city was the Gibson Inn. It towered beside the water. Built in 1907 when the city was in its heyday of lumber mills and commerce, it claimed the skyline at three stories tall, all wrapped in porches that looked out at the water. The Gibson is older now but still a glory to behold. Its beauty mostly speaks of times gone by, a reminder of what the town once was, and a testament to what it could be again. After all, there are all those rooms. Such possibilities.

I was in Apalachicola to give a book reading. The annual Friends of the Library event had become quite a hit, featuring various authors who came to share their stories with locals and visitors alike. The literary world mixing with the landscape. The men in their high-water boots sitting at the bar, smelling of salt, sun, and fresh fish. I had gladly accepted the invitation to be one of the visiting authors, glad for a chance to go "home" again.

While waiting for the event to get underway, I was surprised to see a friend and her husband walk in. Over five hundred miles from where we both lived in Nashville, we were delighted to run into each other. It turned out Mary and Roland Grey had a house on St. George Island nearby. She invited me to join them the following Sunday at their Episcopal church. The church was small and welcoming, reminding me of the chapel I had attended as a girl far out on the west end of Panama City Beach. The taste of salt in the air and the sound of wind slapping and snapping the great, green palm leaves were a comfort.

After the service my friends introduced me to the priest. Somewhere during those few moments over a cup of coffee someone said the name "Iona," and my heart quickened.

"Iona?" I tasted the word on my tongue, noticing how the edges of it felt alive.

The priest said she led a small group to Iona every year on pilgrimage. There was a glow about her eyes as she spoke—one I would come to recognize as the light that name elicits in many. A token of due reverence.

"Take me with you!" I said, not missing a beat. "Really, I want to go."

She told me to call her anytime, and she would share details and dates for the coming year. In the months that followed, I called and left multiple messages. I'm not certain what happened. Maybe she called back to say they had met their quota or that they weren't going that year, and for some reason I didn't receive the message. Or maybe she never called back. Whatever the case, I didn't get to go to Iona that year after all.

But the longing for Iona continued building in me. It didn't grow like the idea of a luxury vacation. Rather, it had the mysterious pull of something else entirely. I just didn't know what. Not yet.

During that time, I had a conversation with the writer Robert Benson, who told me that the power of Iona had reached him too, all the way down in southern Alabama, its influence threading into his life. His wife, a Methodist minister, had visited Iona numerous times, and every time, she brought something of it away with her, something ethereal yet tangible. Although he had never been to Scotland, he felt he had experienced the light of Iona through her. Our conversation reinforced in me the sense of a mystical portal to something I didn't know but longed to touch. Something I longed to see and to test for myself. I sensed I belonged there.

I knew Iona was an island in Scotland, and that according to some references, it was "the birthplace of Celtic Christianity." Beyond that I knew nothing. So I began my research where everyone does nowadays. I googled.

Iona, I read, is one of the outermost islands of Scotland. On the island are the ruins of an old nunnery, a graveyard holding the bones of kings, and an abbey reconstructed on the site of an ancient monastery founded by the Irish monk Columba. This matter is of great importance as it involves the birth of what we know as Celtic Christianity, a mysterious spirituality threaded with history, defeat, and a mystery no one has seemed able to fully unravel.

This longing I began to feel for Iona and for a deeper understanding of Celtic Christianity had no particular basis for being. There was nothing wrong with my own spiritual experience. I was happy with my upbringing in the

Episcopal church. I had also been happy attending nondenominational churches for a number of years. They filled in certain places in my heart, offering an enthusiasm I didn't always find in the more sedate church environment of my growing-up years. But it was the practice of kneeling at the altar for communion, drinking from a common chalice, that I missed most. Eventually, even though my years at a nondenominational church put me in community with some of the warmest and most welcoming people I had ever known, my desire for the sacramental celebration of Holy Communion called to me. A longing for the tradition of my childhood. Growing older and finding comfort in the common things of deep memory. That little Episcopal chapel on the beach. A somber black cross against a white wall. The candlelight service on Christmas Eve. My father still living among us. Yes, perhaps it was this comfort of memory. But still, I longed for deeper waters. For something beyond the veiled curtain. Something I would later describe as more a returning than a finding.

I considered converting to Catholicism. The newly elected Pope Francis was the pope of the working person. No frills, no lace, no waste. These were my people, I said to myself. I called a priest to set up a conference so I could ask him some questions. He never called back.

I shuffled through my mental "rolodex" of mystical branches of the Christian faith: Catholicism, Eastern Orthodox, Greek Orthodox. My friend Scott Cairns is Greek Orthodox, a writer and a learned man of true faith, someone I respect. Also, I had a history with people of Greek ethnicity. I adored them. And since I could pass for Greek, they liked me back. But I didn't convert.

Instead, I whispered the name "Iona," like a clue of some great significance. By now, it had been mentioned to me a dozen times in short succession.

Then I googled something else: the ticket price to Scotland. My heart fell. I didn't have that kind of money.

2

THE SOUND OF SILENCE

THE BLACK LIONS OF Attica once roamed the hills, but now they were extinct.

For years I've carried the cadence of this story with me. On occasion it rises from my subconscious, making itself known again. Recently, I determined to search for the original article about these black lions. I discovered, with a shock, that there never were any great black lions of Attica. It's true that there are a few black-maned lions left in the world. They are glorious to behold, but still, they are not the black lions of Attica, the ones of my imagination that, like some ancient magic, had held me spellbound for so long.

It was the same whenever I heard that word *Iona.* It was always passed along like some secret code. "You simply *must* go to Iona," someone would say. And I would think, *Yes, someday*. But "someday" is a very nebulous timeframe.

I WAS ON ORCAS ISLAND, off the coast of Washington, as a guest in a cottage on the sound, working on a new novel. It's both lovely and lonely to be in such a place on a self-imposed solitary writing sabbatical. It can drive one to distraction and, in some quiet moments, to desperation.

Taking a break from writing, I perused my host's bookshelves, searching for some novel to carry my imagination away. Instead, I was drawn to a small collection of prayers by J. Philip Newell, *Celtic Benediction: Morning and Night Prayer*. I plucked the book up and sat by the window with the afternoon light streaming in over my shoulder, the wild, wicked sound outside all rocks and cold water, and read one of the opening prayers:

> I watch for your light, O God,
> In the eyes of every living creature
> And in the living flame of my own soul.
> If the grace of seeing were mine this day
> I would glimpse you in all that lives.

The prayer goes on to ask for the grace of seeing. It quickened my heart the way reading Rumi does. Only, Newell's words were more connected to the times of my life. More concrete for the moments I was living. I didn't so much read Newell's words as inhale them. There it was—the passionate, prayerful language of the wonder of creation, there on the page. I wanted to know who this man was and why I had just now discovered him.

When I mentioned this author to a friend, he said, "Oh, yes, I know his work. He was warden of Iona Abbey." Of course he was.

A few years later I discovered *Anam Cara* by John O'Donohue. His words sent me tripping gladly over the edge of Celtic Christianity. His understanding of our deepest longings, the language of our souls, the connection and communion we have with other human beings, God, and all of creation spoke to me about the mystery of existence.

Immediately, I decided I would go to Ireland, find O'Donohue, and if he no longer felt called to be a priest and would have me, I'd marry him on the spot. There were only three problems with that plan.

The first: he had recently died.

The second: he had indeed left the priesthood, but had been engaged to be married to his soul mate.

And the third: the entire world felt the same way I did about John O'Donohue. His words sang on the page and in the air. He captured the essence of the mystery that is God, somehow able to make it tangible, accessible, and human, and for that, he was internationally known and beloved.

In learning that this poet and mystic wasn't available, there was nothing left for me to do but explore Celtic Christianity on my own, to make peace with this rattle and hum that came from across the ocean, from a land where I had never been. Wanting to go there, to stand there, shoved out my desire to return first to Italy, where I'd spent time just wandering from city to city on vacation a few years ago. It pushed aside my long-held desire to spend time in the Greek Isles. It stepped large and wide around the beckoning magic of Machu Picchu. It shoved the word *Celtic* straight in front of all other possibilities. I was searching for what Celtic Christians and others call a "thin place," a link between two different worlds. And I believed "Iona" was its name.

My MOTHER MOVED IN with me several years ago. She is in her late eighties but looks much younger. When we go out, beside her I look bedraggled: no makeup, stained jeans, hair unbrushed and in need of a trim. She wears a fashionable scarf, a sassy hat, makeup, jewelry. She is a force to behold. That woman has more fortitude in her little finger than I have ever possessed.

My mother calls herself a flatlander, and this hill that I live on worries her. She can't walk about. She can't plant anything, which has long been her gift—the ability to keep green things alive and growing for longer than a week (which is about my limit). When she first moved here, she looked out around the hill and cried out with lament in her voice, "It's all rock!" She still does that to this day. So I installed window boxes, filling them with flowers for her to tend—an inspiration that soothed her wounded soul, uprooted from her home.

Occasionally, my mother ventures back to north Florida and stays with her niece, my cousin Deb. During one of her little jaunts to enjoy the sun and old friends, I sat alone in my house and pondered. I am a great ponderer once I find my way to the absolute quiet of an empty space. It takes the world coming almost to a full stop for this to happen, but once I arrive at such stillness, I can do this amazing thing: I can stay there. I can be silent for days upon days in a house devoid of noise except, perhaps, the whistling of wind through the eaves and the second-hand ticking of a clock. Now in this near-silence, I thought of the world of Celtic things, and wondered about the sound of the wind blowing across Iona.

I was once silent for forty days. Almost. I met with a spiritual director a few times during that retreat period, but still, that's a lot of quiet. I was also fasting, for the most part. Maybe one protein shake a day. A cup of coffee here and there. But still, that's a lot of skipped meals over forty days. Yet, the amount of arguing and backtalk I have to endure to get to a quiet place is insanely, astronomically ridiculous. And that's just *me* warring with myself over sitting down and shutting up, never mind any other people. In spite of the fact that I know the treasure that waits inside this place of stillness.

In what now feels like another lifetime, I went on several occasions with a few people on retreat to a solitary house on a deserted island. There was no power, just a small gas stove and propane lanterns for light. We arrived by boat and, depending on the weather, were dropped off on the lagoon side of the house. Or if the seas were calm enough, we would jump overboard and, our packs over our heads, wade to the shore and down the beach to the house. With great ceremony we took off our watches and placed them in a closet, refusing to look at them or retrieve them until the sun had set and risen again for however many days we were afforded. It was always at least three, sometimes more. We declared that we had left "man-made time" and entered "island time," which I considered "God time."

On the first day of a retreat, a kind of giddiness ensued. What should we do first? Walk on the beach? Search for turtle eggs? Count the huge number of pelicans flying in with their day's catch? Build a sandcastle? Play cards? We rushed from one delightful activity to the next. But by the first night, when the sun had set and the waves were steadily rolling to shore, we grew quieter. By the second day, our words became fewer, and when spoken, they were softer. If one of us woke in the night, we wandered to the porch, sat in a rocker, and watched the moonlight on the waves until we were lulled by the rhythm of the light and the tide back to bed. By the third day, we barely spoke at all. Each day felt like it held forty-eight hours, and every hour doubled in on itself, divided, and multiplied. Time stretched into more time. With a peaceful, slow companionship we watched the birds, sketched sea oats and sand dunes, and finally came into a blessed rhythm that allowed us to hear ourselves think.

Now, in the absence of my mother and our normal routine I had space to *think*. I mean no ill in that. My mother and I have our fun, but with the constant companionship, the noise of conversation, the to-dos of caretaking, my thinking slides into a small box. With each passing day of schedules, medicines, and meals—one, two, three—the box gets smaller still. Grocery stores and appointments, phone calls and concerns. The box shrinks down to the tiniest space until my thoughts are only words, and not all choice ones.

When I've reached this point, it takes three full days of absolute silence for the boxes to begin to open and thoughts to surface in proper order for me to even begin to touch the center of who I am and who God is in me. Three days is a long time, a lot of silence. It's an eternity. To turn off phones and television and streaming devices. To not medicate myself by binge-watching a series of my latest liking. It takes simply being still. There is nothing about our modern world, particularly American culture, that supports this stillness. It is anathema to our society. Yet, it is the thing I must return to, this solace of silence.

The view from my hill is all trees and branches, birds and squirrels, and the shadow and light that play in and around them all. I can see from this ridge clear across a little valley to the ridge on the other side. If I stand on my little porch and look just so and squint, well, then I can see for miles and miles. Kevin, my large rescue dog who is part mutt and part Pyrenees, all fine fur and dirt, takes up residence on the couch much of the day. After guarding the hill all night, he likes to come in at morning light and suffer himself a little comfort. He falls deep asleep and, eventually, snores in the way of big, old dogs, low and soft and sure. I'll take that sound to my grave, clutching it to my chest; I swear I will.

On this day, I sat in the old chair, looked out the window at the trees, and pondered for hours. What came to me in that clear, quiet space was that I didn't want to just *go* to Iona; I wanted to touch the light I had seen reflected in the eyes of those who'd gone before me whenever they spoke of it. And when I did manage to touch that light, I wanted to capture the moment in story. Never mind that I had a mystery series in the works and an old Southern gothic novel I'd been wanting to finish for years. Iona was calling.

What had once been a whisper now became a craving for some unseen place, for an unknown reason. And because of this one moment when I arrived at the center of my quietness and felt I could indeed, as J. Philip Newell writes, "hear the heartbeat of God," I knew that writing a book about Celtic Christianity was precisely what I was meant to do. I suspected the hand of God in this business. Outside, the wind picked up, bustled the tree branches, and gusted across the porch. And for just a moment, I thought I heard bells.

3

THE ANCESTORS OF TOTALITY

LAST CHRISTMAS MY SON Chris had my DNA tested because he wanted to know more about his ancestral heritage. Although I knew I had Irish genes, I didn't realize the test would pinpoint the precise location of my roots. When the DNA results included a map of Ireland that revealed specifically where my ancestors were from, I felt a deeper connection with that history. This was where the ancient Celtic people had been, the place from which Irish monks had wandered their way north to what would one day be Iona.

I took comfort in knowing my ancestors had walked the holy ground I longed for. It was as if, by digging deep into the Celtic past, I would find their stone circles, their markers, their ruins. In doing so, I imagined I might even discover the secret of how to integrate the very presence of God into my life, to be enriched with power, passion, and purpose. It felt as if, through this connection, I would even be able to tap into the same source that gave us galaxies. To carry that light within me and keep it shining. To abide in that time that is outside the realm of humanity but easily within the grasp of God.

But the quandary was that I was between book events. Tracing my finger back and forth on the calendar, I flipped months ahead and thought, "What if?" and, "Just maybe . . ." Then my cup of frustration spilled over and became fear. "What if I can't make it there? To the Celtic homeland? To Iona? What kind of book will this be if I must simply write it based on research and interviews?" But I answered myself aloud, "No, that would be a horrible book. A very bad, horrible book."

I stepped out onto my porch in the midst of my deadlines and impossibilities, all collected into a perfect storm in my soul that was downright worrisome. How could I possibly write this book about Celtic spirituality and get it right? And in those few minutes of sunshine, a butterfly landed on a flower in the window box and I was captivated, transported into a world of magic and mystery. The blue butterfly drank from the red burst of petals I had planted for my mother. And my small act of selfless love offered back to me that day its beauty as a gift. I had given energy to bring something to life, and it had returned life to me. Creation to creation.

The butterfly took flight, immediately replaced by a bee that found its way to the center of each flower. I watched the weight of him, lazy and satisfied, as he lifted off, landed, lifted off, landed. Several hummingbirds churned their wings above me. The cicadas sang in waves, their sound rising and falling with the wind. It was all an orchestrated, sweet ode to summer.

This was the music that the Celtic people brought to Christianity. A wildness that dared to erase the preconceived boundaries of God's existence. While history shows that the Celts welcomed and embraced Christianity, they made this new knowledge of God their own, weaving it into the fabric of what they already held sacred, not missing a beat in the process. Their beliefs, which were considered pagan by the Romans, were deeply connected to nature, the seasons, and the cycles of life—indeed, to God's creation.

All of which I witnessed while I paused on the porch, trying to catch my breath from the insanity of the life I had created for myself. The very life that threatened some days to engulf me. The pressures I'd brought into my house. My list of goals and things to accomplish that complicated my existence. All of this, I realized now, had brought turbulence between me and the presence of God, like static from a radio not tuned in to the right frequency.

Yet as I stood on this hill I call home, in this space surrounded by trees, with its view over the little valley to the ridge beyond—this space alive with nature began to heal me. And part of the healing came as I remembered a day in August 2017, when a historic event cast darkness across parts of the United States and encapsulated Nashville: a total solar eclipse.

For a long time beforehand, I was oblivious, head down, busy working. I was not aware the eclipse was on its way until I began to hear people talking about it in stores and purchasing special glasses. There was additional buzz about how many people would suddenly arrive in Nashville because we were in the direct path of totality—the eclipse's complete darkness.

Sometimes I need to listen to the small voice that is the songline of my soul. To hear the whisper of "This way, follow me." For some it is the voice of God, for others their sixth sense. For me it is both; I see them as one and the same.

Fifteen years ago, I moved to Nashville following that voice. That's the short and simple version of the story, but it was that clear. It had to be Nashville. No other place on a large map filled with other places. I knew no one in the city, had no relatives in the area, and had no job lined up. Yet, Nashville was where I knew I had to be. I'd never regretted following that voice, and I was more certain than ever on that Monday a few short years ago when the celestial bodies aligned.

A few weeks before the eclipse I finally realized this major cosmic event was headed my way. Or that I was headed toward it.

Nashville had scheduled huge watch events with outdoor concerts. Stores sold out of eclipse-watching sunglasses, ordered more, sold out again. I didn't buy any. I bought Guinness. There was that small instinctual voice again. *Alone*, it whispered. So, alone I would be, I thought. I would follow that songline and sit on my porch, watch and wait with expectation, and experience the unknown all by myself.

I woke up that morning and said aloud to myself, "Eclipse Day!" as if it were Christmas morning. I worked on a short story about a woman waiting for an eclipse. Then the refrigerator repairman showed up. I had forgotten about him. Nervously, I checked the official "scoundrel time" and told him that the penumbra was coming. He asked, "What's a penumbra?" When I told him, he said, "Well, that explains it."

All the roads were almost completely blocked by then because people had simply stopped their cars to watch. I told him he could take a Guinness with him, but that I had to focus on the eclipse. Alone.

I love the light that passes through the filter of leaves encircling my house—large oaks and elms and hickories. I love the sun on their bark, the fog that weaves among their limbs in the early morning. I have a relationship with these woods. So I sat on my tiny front porch, watching the light change in the trees as the shadows shifted forward.

I opened a beer. (My philosophy is that God made Guinness—with a little help from the Irish!—so there was no better drink for that event on that day.) I would drink to my Irish ancestors who had walked the very ground where, some five thousand years ago on what came to be known as November 30 and St. Andrew's Day (Scotland's official national day), the ancient Irish carved an eclipse into a stone now called "Cairn L," just outside Kells, in County Meath, Ireland. This felt to me like more than just a token of all things aligning—it felt downright divine.

I noticed the singing of the cicadas and birds. Dogs barked off in the distance down the hill. It was the middle of the day, but night was falling, the shadows lengthening. There was the slightest breeze, and I felt the heavy-handed heat of the southern August day lift. Daylight began to bow to the passing moon.

I watched this approaching night for the hours it unfolded and then, at the speed of atoms splitting, like a rogue wave, totality crashed over me. It was as if a thousand keys unlocked a thousand doors at once and forever. I jumped to my feet and whispered, *"Jesus, Jesus, Jesus"*—not in fear or in prayer, but in awe. Wonderstruck. To be alive at that moment, in the path of that occurrence, and experiencing it in such an intimate way.

During the zenith of the darkness, I stepped out onto the uncovered landing of the porch and looked up at the sky where the stars had appeared. Not gradually, not a handful, but a skyful! All of them at once. Midnight stars. The birds and cicadas fell silent, while crickets woke up and began their evening song. Fireflies danced all around me.

Then ever so slowly, day slid out from under the moon again. It swept across the yard, shadows chased away by light until the full sun returned. Cheers erupted from a crowd of eclipse watchers miles away, and the sound lasted a long, long time.

Late that afternoon I watched the NASA coverage featuring interviews with people from across the nation about this moment so exciting, so breathtaking, so unifying. And the following day I was in a Nashville bookstore filled with visitors who had traveled for miles and now were drawn to the store in search of books about eclipses. Strangers made eye contact and asked, "Did you see it? Were you there?" Then everyone began sharing stories of where they'd been as they watched.

One man from Texas looked at me with a deeply serious expression and said, "Totality is everything."

"Yes," I said.

"Ninety percent isn't good enough," he continued, adamant about this.

"No, sir," I said. "It's totality or nothing at all."

Another man looked over and said, "Me and my wife had to run from the clouds up in Kentucky. We just kept on driving 'til the sun came out."

"Is that a fact?"

"Yes, but we made it, and when we crossed over into Tennessee, it was clear, and we just got off the interstate and pulled off at the first place we could find."

"It was a field behind the JCPenney," the woman said, and I guessed she was the wife. "It was full of people already. Everybody was there to watch." Then she added, with her eyes full of the same wonder I had experienced, "It was perfect."

"There was an Indian man that had come all the way down from New York City," said the man, taking over the telling again. "And I was watching the whole thing, and he was standing right next to us, and he had his hand held over his heart the whole time. When it was all over, and the sun came out, he told me, 'Where I come from, in my religion, this is a spiritual experience.' I told him, 'Buddy, I come down from Kentucky, and it's a spiritual experience for me too.'" Then the couple exchanged tired, road-weary, happy smiles.

Another man stopped browsing the bookshelf and joined the conversation. "You know, for just a minute we all stopped fighting. It wasn't about politics or arguing. We were all in the same place. Suddenly we were all on the same page."

Yes, I thought. *That was it. Once again. On television, on the streets, in the stores. For a moment, we had become one people again.*

Then everyone started opening the eclipse books, searching for their next eclipse pilgrimage. Marking the trajectory of the sun, the earth, the moon. "Argentina," a woman said, speaking up for the first time. "I was born there and haven't been back in thirty years, but I'm going for this."

The world has its scoffers, people who might ask, "What is all the noise about? Big deal. Sun, moon, eclipse— I get it." And then other people, a little lukewarm, might say, "Well, that was an interesting show; now let's get back to business." But there's another group of people, the ones who experienced the event and were deeply affected when those celestial bodies aligned, who felt an awakening of bold illumination, who heard the music of the spheres as we moved in ordinary time, circling the sun and each other with a divine purpose.

My ancient Celtic ancestors had also, no doubt, turned their faces toward the sky in wonder at an event they surely didn't understand, but that meant so much to them that they carved its image into stone. The people who existed there before anyone was known as "Celtic" had left the old-est known record of an eclipse, and I know without question that they experienced the same incredible awe of the moment that I did. Perhaps they felt, too, that not even the blink of an eye stood between us. We travel together through this vast universe in this corridor of time, and that is the greatest miracle of all.

THAT SUMMER AFTERNOON, AS I tried to sort out my calendar to make a transatlantic journey possible . . . as I stood on my porch surrounded by nature with its cacophony of sounds . . . as I looked up at the same trees that had cast silent silver shadows during the eclipse . . . I was slowed. Hushed. Healed. I inhabited a world filled with the vibration of living things and planetary wonders. For those few sweet moments I didn't worry about the price of flights or the impossible things that had to come to pass for me to set out on a pilgrimage to Iona.

Quaker pastor and writer Brent Bill says it is the Quakers' old custom, when leaving a friend, to say, "I'll see you again when way opens."

A way would have to reveal itself where there was no way at all. I couldn't control all those details any more than I could control the cicadas or choreograph the revolution of planets around the sun. So I watched the cobalt blue of the butterfly's wings stroking the air as it returned, and took flight again, and I wondered if that blue might match the skies over Iona.

4

An *Anam cara* For THe Trip

My TRAVELS HAVE RUN the gamut from five-star to rustic, from solo trips to adventures with friends.

Road trips are among my favorite things to do, my prescription for shucking off troubles that settle in and seem to have nowhere else to go, like a dark cloud hanging over my house. I know the answer to that: get in a car and drive until the cloud is in the rearview mirror and the sun comes out. Until the air grows warmer and I can roll down the windows, let the wind whip through my hair, and keep on driving until the stars come out in a blue-black sky. With every mile, life gets better, troubles fall away, and answers come more easily.

I am comfortable in my solitude, and am even better company for myself on a long stretch of road. I've traveled solo across the vast wilds of America. One particular journey I enjoy is crossing along the Gulf Coast, through Texas, and north toward Tucumcari, New Mexico. There I pick up an old state road and travel through a landscape of mesas and mystery. Eventually I reach the high desert and the city of Taos. Being alone heightens the experience of each lightning bolt, every shooting star, the wafting night scent of piñon, and the desert filled with blooming chamisa.

When my days become stressful, when I need more room to think, I long for the open desert, long to travel the road to Santa Fe and watch the setting sun turn the Sangre de Cristo Mountains the color indicated by their name— "the blood of Christ" in Spanish.

As I tried to sort out the quandary of getting to Scotland, I wanted to kick around for a few days near the Four Corners (where New Mexico, Arizona, Utah, and Colorado meet), an area brimming with history and the mystery of the Anasazi, whom the Navajo people call "the ancient ones." I wanted to wander up the mountain to Taos Pueblo, where I'd gone once for Christmas Eve mass, the Taos culture and traditions blending so beautifully. There a raging bonfire burned, and we warmed ourselves as the snow fell.

Taos is the site of one of the oldest pueblos (indigenous settlements) in the United States and one of the few continuously occupied for a thousand years. The people and their landscape have pulled on me since the moment, years ago, when my car first crossed into Tucumcari and the wild West opened up as if I were traveling back in time. Now, I wanted to get behind the wheel and point my car in that direction. Just one long drive through the night and into morning, and I'd be able to walk in the paths of these ancient ones, feel the echo of their footsteps, and surely discover the answers to my questions.

As much as I enjoyed traveling solo, having a trusted friend along for a journey doubled the fun. Someone who knew me well, inside and out. A person who knew my faults and frailties to the bone and would either point them out to me or pat me on the back and say, "That's you being you," depending on the situation. In other words, someone who could both provide wise counsel and have a damn good time—characteristics that don't always come in one package. I am blessed with many friends from various corners of my life, but only a handful possess precisely this set of criteria. What's more, the demands of life don't allow my friends and me to spend as much time together as we'd like.

But one friend close enough to be considered a "soul friend"—what the Celts call an *anam cara*—is my sister. The Celtic Christians put a lot of stock in this concept, practically making it a requirement. Everyone needs someone to fill this role in their life, they concluded, because life is for the long game and requires someone to help you make the right decisions along the way—a friend who knows you intimately.

My little sister was born when I was seven years old, and I was happy to no longer be an only child. I took her with me everywhere, even on dates when I became a teenager, and we have remained inseparably close all our lives. Even now she lives down the street from me, having moved to Nashville a few years after I did. As much as she would have loved to go to Scotland and I'd adore her being there, the demands of her work schedule and having two teenagers in school didn't make an international trip on short notice possible for her.

Another of my soul friends is my cousin Deb, who has gotten me both into and out of trouble more times than I can count. Our travels are always a grand adventure, and our last long-distance road trip took us from the rain forests to the beaches of Costa Rica. But cousin Deb loves five-star hotels and the essentials one might discover at an exclusive spa. And the journey to Scotland I was about to set out on wasn't going to include facials and pedicures.

I once spent an unforgettable week on a press trip to Montreal, where I was hosted at the Queen Elizabeth Hotel. The beautiful woman behind the gorgeous desk took my name and said, "Oh, you're on seventeen." Then she gave me a special key to reach the VIP floor, made famous by John Lennon and Yoko Ono's second bed-in protest against the war in Vietnam.

My mornings began with the hotel's version of a six o'clock wakeup call: a gentle knock at my door and a soft, accented "Bonjour, Mademoiselle," as the nice room-service waiter brought my strong coffee in on a silver tray. Then I sat in a robe thick and soft as angels' wings, sipping the dark brew and gazing out as the sunrise broke the horizon and illuminated the dome of the Mary, Queen of the World Cathedral. I considered the blessings of God and how far I'd roamed. Deb would have loved being with me on that trip. Fine dining and luxury at every turn.

A few weeks later I was back in the States, en route to the Wild Goose Festival for a speaking engagement. Upon arrival, I was informed that my reservation had been lost and my room booked to someone else. So I climbed in the back of my jeep, unrolled the sleeping bag I kept for emergencies, and went to sleep. The next morning, I washed my face with water from my water bottle, used the top-notch facilities of the portable toilet, grabbed a coffee, and went on stage to speak on the subject of divine possibilities, the value of community, and the importance of human connection.

Flexibility and a certain no-frills, down-to-earth sensibility can come in handy on the road. And making a pilgrimage to Iona was going to require a certain cowgirl can-do attitude. My friend Virginia can travel like that: carrying a pack and sleeping in the forest. She is as fearless as she is faithful. I have known her since seventh grade, and we have weathered the ups and downs of life with a sense of humor and prayerful hope. I dialed her number in Oregon. On the third ring she picked up.

"I'm going on a quest to Scotland," I said. "It'll be hard. I have no money. We'll have to carry what we need in only the packs on our backs. And one more thing—I don't know how we'll eat or where we'll sleep."

"When do we leave?" was her only response. No questions. No qualifiers. No maybes.

So against the odds and without the means, we turned our minds toward Scotland, scrolled through the calendars on our phones, and searched for optimal dates. The sooner the better, we decided. "You should really go to Scotland in the springtime," friends had said, "when the weather is up for it." So we decided we'd go in May or, at the latest, early June.

Then May came and went, and the days stretched into summer. The Scotland plan was postponed indefinitely. In keeping with my lifestyle, it was going to take a wing and a prayer to get there.

5

THE SYNERGY
OF BREAD CRUMBS

In APRIL 2019 MY book *Confessions of a Christian Mystic* came out. Visits with bookstores soon filled my calendar. May came and went with a quickness. Then June arrived and followed suit. There were dates to speak at book shops and book signings. I packed my bags and prepared myself to hit the road. This was my familiar. Years of this writing business had given me so many great experiences, and the joy of meeting readers face-to-face instead of just online never grew stale. Only this time, I needed to be in two places at once. Between every stop along the way, I tracked airfares to Scotland and worked at pulling a plan together.

At five a.m. three days before I was set to take off for my first engagement, a brown recluse spider bit me in the crook of my arm. I knew this because I snapped my eyes open, sat up wide awake with a stinging pain in my arm, and turned on the light, all the while thinking, *A brown recluse spider has just bitten me!* I threw back the covers and there was said spider trying to make a quick getaway before the book on my bedside table popped him so that he was surely dead but still identifiable. By six a.m. my arm was throbbing and burning. At seven a.m. I had a conference call. At 7:30 I had the spider corpse in a tiny matchbox and was on the way to the doctor. They asked me, "Exactly why do you think it was a brown recluse?" I presented the dead spider in its matchbox coffin. They concluded that, yes, I had indeed been bitten by the horrible brown recluse. And they were impressed that I had the presence of mind to capture the spider without making him into something beyond recognition.

By that evening my arm had started turning black. The doctor increased the dose of my antibiotics to triple strength. My sister put me on her church's prayer chain. Readers prayed for me, nuns prayed for me, my mother prayed for me. I put my suitcase in the car with creams and wraps and ointments and antibiotics and hit the road. What else can a cowgirl do but saddle up and ride?

I stopped at a friend's house in Asheville, North Carolina, on my way to South Carolina for a literary luncheon on St. Pawleys Island. Asheville is a beautiful place, and my friend is an old playwrighting buddy from way back when. It was good to catch up and spend time relaxing, to sip wine and talk about books, including the new one I was writing. I told him all about my dreams of making it to Iona and about the history of Celtic Christianity.

When I took my suitcase to the car, there was a six-foot-long, big, black snake crawling up on the undercarriage of my car. I kid you not. I have pictures to prove it. So with my arm wrapped up in ointment, taking my antibiotics, I pulled into a place that did oil changes and asked them if they would please put my car up so they could search for the snake. I am not afraid of snakes. I don't like them, however, and what I like even less is the potential surprise of a snake climbing over my shoulder while I'm going around a mountain along the Blue Ridge Parkway. There was no sign of the snake, who was possibly curled up out of reach, or I had flung him off as I drove wild donuts in the parking lot trying to get him loose.

People told me things during this time. Sometimes friends would say I was under attack by evil forces. Or sometimes they would just laugh and say, "*Only you* can start out on a book tour like this." Some people were speechless. I believe strongly in that old adage that the show must go on. I have the theatre in my blood—it's where my professional writing began, where I discovered my voice, if you will—and with that attitude came a whole lot of Southern-girl rural survival backbone. So I pulled on my seven-year-old boots from Tractor Supply, wrapped gauze around an ice bag on my left arm, and drove off, keeping one eye constantly looking for any sign of something that might slither its way over my seat.

Once I actually made it to St. Pawleys Island with no sign of the snake, I had the lovely opportunity to stay with a dear friend and her family. It was all saltwater and marshes, and it's some of the most beautiful land I've ever seen. Linda's porch had a beautiful view of the yard that rambled down to an inlet that led out to the bay and eventually to the Atlantic Ocean. She's a cancer survivor, inspirational speaker, and writer, and I'm thankful for the multitude of dots in my life that have connected my story with hers. She took one look at my arm and said, "I hope you'll stay long enough that I can take you to our church for the healing service on Wednesday."

As I sat on her porch, her daughter Chloe, home for a visit, greeted me with her normal, precious enthusiasm. She's a light in this world, Chloe is. We settled down for a talk about her studies and my work. When she asked me what my new project was, I told her, "A book on Celtic Christianity." And precious Chloe turned to gold before my eyes.

"Oh, River! I studied Celtic Christianity in Scotland and went to all the sites. And, oh, *Iona*. You have to go, River! You just have to go to Iona."

She ran upstairs and gathered all of the textbooks from her course. "I knew I was saving them for a reason." She showed me each title, discussing them with me and showing me the ones that were her favorites.

Then I asked her, "Why Iona, Chloe? Of all the sites you went to, what was it about that island in particular?"

That Iona look came over her. The same one I'd seen in the eyes of the Episcopal priest.

"There is," she paused, "the light. Definitely, the light is something special. Like, it has a tangible quality. An essence of its own."

We spoke for an hour about her travels and experiences. Then she offered me something else: her opinion that some people travel all the way to Iona, and they arrive, but they still don't get it. They don't see what others see. They don't sense the presence of those layers upon layers of prayers laid down for so many years. "There is nothing special at all about Iona to them," Chloe said. "And it just hurts me for them that they were standing right there, on holy ground, and they didn't get it at all."

I stayed for the Wednesday service, then I returned home to Nashville, unpacked the car, immediately made a cup of coffee, and spread the books out before me. I read of armies and wars, conquests and betrayals. Of people who once believed in the *genius loci*, or the spirit of the place. It was a time of many gods and also of great superstition, curses, and dark spells. War and magic. Intrigue and suspicion. Politics and poison. I read until my eyes grew weary, and I fell asleep thinking of pilgrimages.

IN SPITE OF MY Celtic encounter with Chloe, the trip seemed to keep growing farther and farther away instead of closer. It was always one thing or another. One month, finances delayed our departure, then another bookstore visit or my mother's medical appointments.

In lieu of leaving, I picked up two more books on the history of Celtic Christianity, read them, and added more notes to my notes. I was getting a lot of note-taking done but was not doing the writing I wanted that would incorporate firsthand experiences like Chloe's.

There are dreams and there are destinies, and sometimes they cross over to become one and the same thing. If so, journeying on pilgrimage to Iona was as much God's plan as it was mine, which meant we were in this thing together. And if that was so, I hoped God's plan was coming together better than mine. In the meantime, I said nothing of this plan to travel to Scotland to my mother. Why worry her with this thing when I didn't have the details down? And she had enough on her mind, as she was still checking my black-and-blue spider-bite arm for signs of it healing.

A few days later as I was mulling over options in my mind, I followed my mother around in a bookstore. She was searching for some book she really wanted, but now she couldn't remember the title. Thinking maybe if we perused the aisles together she'd see something that would jog her memory, we walked up and down all of the aisles until we accidentally wandered down one that displayed Bibles. We were both drawn to one small edition with a soft, green cover that featured the Celtic sign of the Trinity, encircled by a Celtic weaving. More Celtic scrollwork was imprinted all along the border.

"I've never seen a Bible like this one," my mother said. I agreed with her: neither had I. She held it and turned it over, weighed it in her hands. "I want it," she declared as if that had been her reason for the trip to the store. Later that night, deciding the print was too small for her, she gifted it to me.

One of the first pages of the Bible explained the publisher's approach to this version: "Bible translation is both a science and an art. It is a bridge that brings God's Word from the ancient world to the world today."

The actor, singer, and writer John Schneider calls these moments "God-winks"—and explained to me that when these God winks happen, they let him know he's headed in the right direction.

I call these little occurrences bread crumbs on the path. Like John's God-winks, they let me know I'm traveling, the right direction.

I had lots of Celtic research books, a Bible with its Celtic cover, I was inked with a Celtic tattoo. And I also had an *anam cara*, a soul friend lined up for the journey. None of these things added up to an authentic Celtic spirituality, but they each meant something to me, and that was a good beginning. Now I just needed those tickets.

I reread my O'Donohue books, including *Walking in Wonder*, a collection of radio engagements published posthumously. I read books about Celtic Christian history and spirituality by Esther De Waal and J. Philip Newell. I reread *Holy Rover* by Lori Erickson, underlining the chapters about Iona. I read spiritual offerings like *To Hear the Forest Sing*, musings on the divine by Margaret Dulaney, and *New Seeds of Contemplation* by Thomas Merton.

I paced in my room, tracing a mental finger through the days, weeks, and months that were flying by. I called Virginia and said, "Soon, somehow we'll get tickets and begin this journey." But as I said it, I wondered if that was the truth or if this would possibly never happen.

Oh, yes, and I prayed.

THE FOLLOWING MORNING I went to an Episcopal church in a neighborhood of the city I was in and asked if the church was open for prayer. I was told that the main sanctuary was not, but that the chapel down the hallway was available.

I searched silent hallways and passed classrooms. I passed a little open-air bookstore with a poster showing how to purchase items on the honor system. Eventually, I found my way to the chapel. Candles flickered from previous visitors. I imagined them making personal pleas for themselves or family members experiencing a rough go of it or maybe just a grateful prayer of thanksgiving. I lit a candle and added mine to theirs. Then I also included a petition for their needs, these strangers who had come before me. We were kindred souls, whoever and wherever they were. Like me, they had come to the altar this morning seeking something we reached for by faith.

On my way out, I stopped by the bookstore, searching for anything on the practices of Celtic Christianity, but was soon distracted by a display of Anglican prayer beads. I was drawn to one strand in particular, the only one with a Celtic cross. The card that accompanied them read, "These particular beads were fashioned with the Celtic way in mind." I bought them straightaway. Included with the beads was a list of prayers, and when I read the one attributed to St. Patrick, tears filled my eyes; the words pulled on my heart. The prayer read like something I'd been trying to say for a long time.

A group of children filled the hallway, marching single file. For the most part. At four or five years old, straight lines are a challenge. They were off to the chapel for rehearsal for their St. Patrick's Day performance. I clutched my new beads and St. Patrick's prayer. I thought of the way that things could spiritually align, all at once coming together in such a way that I knew I was indeed following the songline, the path that was calling me. I stood and waited there in the hallway until the children began to sing, lifting their small voices up to God in hymns unknown to me but Irish in their origin.

Following the spiritual bread crumbs laid out before me, I was met with a banquet of zigs and zags and improbabilities that led me to the exact spot at the precise time that I was meant to be, even if for some reason unknown to me.

I had to go to Iona. A way had to open. And I had no idea how that was going to happen.

I kept studying and writing and searching maps online, alternately checking airfares. I found a Norwegian discount flight for some ridiculous price advertised in the *New York Times* travel section for two hundred and something dollars round-trip. The only catch was to get to New York. And back again and to find friends or money for overnights in New York coming and going, and all my configurations didn't seem to make it possible. Sometimes following God is like trying to decipher spiritual hieroglyphics, and I wanted special glasses that would let me magically see the full future laid out before me. Instead I received my daily bread, one bread crumb, one day at a time. The trick was, I had to just trust and keep following.

I began praying the St. Patrick's Breastplate Prayer every day. I carried the prayer beads with me everywhere, in my pocket, my purse, my robe. I misplaced them as frequently as I carried them and felt at odds and out of sorts when they went missing. Saying the prayer was my place of beginning, and when I arrived at the part of the prayer that held up the glory of creation, it simultaneously grounded me in the natural realm of the earth and washed me in wonder at the realm of God. This was a good place to begin a moment, to listen and begin my day.

I bind unto myself today
the virtues of the starlit heaven,
the glorious sun's life-giving ray,
the whiteness of the moon at even,
the flashing of the lightning free,
the whirling of the winds' tempestuous shocks,
the stable earth, the deep salt sea,
around the old eternal rocks.

From there I would go on to pray for my friends and loved ones, for Facebook friends and requests, for peace on earth, and so on and so forth.

Without those beads, I sometimes rushed headlong into my days, missing the divine call. But it was amazing how by using them in my spiritual discipline, I slowed to be more present. Things didn't always go as smoothly or in as inspired a way as I hoped. There were hiccups. But little by little I was learning. More and more, I wrapped my fingers around that Celtic cross, beads in hand, and began my day with the words of St. Patrick's Breastplate Prayer.

I bind unto myself today
the strong name of the Trinity
by invocation of the same, three in one and one in
    three,
by whom all Creation has its being.

6

THE BOOK OF KELLS

I HAD BEEN SEARCHING ONLINE for all things Celtic for so long that it was only a matter of time until the little tech gods of algorithms popped up with information about an Irish Celtic jeweler. It was perfect clickbait, and I went for it. I popped into the site for an Irish jeweler who made beautiful Celtic crosses, and then I saw a wedding band that featured scrollwork from the famous ancient *Book of Kells*. I promised myself this ring if I should ever remarry. Surely a ring such as this would promise a fairytale of a happy ending.

I jokingly told friends that as far as I was concerned, someday in the distant future I could get married in a pub over a pint of Guinness to the first man who sat down and spoke up about theoretical physics and how it all tied in with Divinity. Recognizing immediately that we were twin flames, I'd ask him to marry me, and he'd say yes, and the wedding rings of *The Book of Kells* would magically appear from behind the bar as a priest walked in to order a pint. Alas, my life is likely not to unfold this way. And 'tis a shame, that.

The Book of Kells has long held my fascination. Considered by experts and pilgrims to be the most beautiful book on earth, its appeal is deep and wide. A historian would appreciate it as one of the rare preserved books featuring the calligraphy and artwork of the Middle Ages. From a writer's perspective, the amount of time that went into painstakingly creating the book is a wonder in itself: words lovingly treasured and recreated, ornately designed, and preserved. The fact that the most beautiful book in the world contains the story of Christ as told by his disciples would make the trip to see it a holy pilgrimage in itself. For those who identify with all things Celtic, the intricate weavings, complete with the tiniest details of animals and trees and Celtic scrollwork throughout, are objects of great interest. For those simply drawn to beautiful things, *The Book of Kells* stands out in its excellence the way the Sistine Chapel is central to the art world. People often wonder how humankind could possibly create these objects. Was it through the help of angels? The breath of God?

I was fascinated by the artwork of *The Book of Kells* and appreciated it for all these reasons. And I knew a few simple facts about the book: It had been created by monks using special inks in a rich array of colors from various exotic, foreign lands. In a time when no jets filled the skies and travel of any distance was rare and limited, it's a mystery how the monks managed to procure costly rare inks from around the world. And yet, the magical *Book of Kells* was created.

The four volumes that comprise *The Book of Kells* are now housed at Trinity College in Dublin, where millions of people make pilgrimage each year to view it. Two books are always displayed at one time—one that features the artwork and one that features the calligraphy of the Latin text.

What I didn't know until later was that the origin of the book and the site of its creation was the Isle of Iona. The monks who painstakingly made this work were Columba's monks in that first monastery of Celtic Christianity. The book escaped Iona just before the last Viking raid in which sixty-four monks were murdered, all the holy relics looted, and the monastery burned to the ground. It was later discovered hidden in County Meath in Ireland, when it was then officially named *The Book of Kells*.

So the precious *Book of Kells* had originated on what I began to think of now as "my" Isle of Iona. But on that day as I surfed the Celtic-jewelry website, I wasn't getting married in a pub or even dating, so marriage looked unlikely. I passed on the wedding rings and ordered the little silver Celtic cross. Then I made another note in my research journal: "Must see *The Book of Kells*."

7

THE DIRTY WORK
OF HOLY BUSINESS

AT FIRST GLANCE THE words *Celtic Christianity* seem heavily weighted toward the "Celtic" part, light on the "Christian." For some, that may be the initial attraction. The perfume, a heady mix of *Highlander*, *Braveheart*, and magical stones that seemed as though they would allow us to travel through time. But those desiring a romantic version of this tradition might proceed with caution. Not all from the history volumes of Celtic Christianity was first kiss, first love, first light. The history of Celtic Christianity is filled with violence, Viking raids, murdered monks, and destroyed monasteries. It is overrun with political turmoil and argument, fear and misunderstandings. And yet, through it all, the vein of Christianity that came up the Irish coast to Scotland survived and spread far beyond the island where it first took hold. It's what spoke to me, but I didn't forget that it came at a great price and much sacrifice.

IN 563 AN IRISH monk named Columba left Ireland with twelve disciples and traveled by boat along the coast of Scotland. He was on a self-imposed exile from Ireland (the details would fill another book). Ultimately, he settled on the westernmost island, the Isle of Iona, and there founded a monastery. The island is only three miles long and one mile wide. It is difficult to reach, remote and disconnected from the mainland. In spite of how small and how remote, it was as if the land itself had a destiny and worked alongside Columba to fulfill it. This isle would become a medieval center of Christian influence.

Then came a meeting between representatives of two traditions of the growing Christian church that became a bit of a theological shoot-out. The meeting was known as the Synod of Whitby.

One tradition held up as their symbol the image of St. John, the disciple who leaned against the breast of Jesus at the Last Supper and was therefore considered the only disciple who heard the heartbeat of God. This tribe believed that listening to the heartbeat, through stillness and contemplation and the celebration of all creation, was the way to commune with the Creator. In belief and nature, they were Celtic.

The second tradition was just as passionate in their beliefs, and this group held up as their symbol the image of St. Peter. They taught that the foundation of faith and following Christ meant acts of service and operating within the structure of organized religious worship, and teachings from Scriptures by appointed leaders. In thought and belief, they were Roman.

The Whitby meeting was meant to accomplish something in the way of an agreement between them. Many of the attendees sought a compromise between these factions and hoped the meeting would serve to bring them closer together. Regardless of what the intent was for good or bad, political or spiritual, what evolved was that the Roman version of the faith that looked to St. Peter won out. It became the official faith of the land and, in so doing, pushed the more mystical of the two to the fringes of Britain, where it remained.

And yet the story, as all good stories do, holds a surprise. The Celtic form of Christianity remained and flourished and today draws many seekers—both Christians and those who hail from other faith traditions. People who find interest in this form of spirituality are drawn to it for its embrace of the wildness of God and its way of seeking the Creator in all of creation.

Each of those two groups who saw their world and faith differently argued over which way would be best for the Christian faith to move forward. There are many documented factors that influenced this division, but the one that interests me is the discomfort the Roman-church supporters felt at how Celtic Christians so easily absorbed some of the mysticism of the pre-Christian Celtic and Druid people. Strange they were, and strange they stayed. And in this tug-of-war over ideals and practices, it appeared that the belief system that featured more of the St. John history was overruled. It would be Rome, they decided, that in the tradition of Peter, would be the formal seat of the church and would dictate how Christianity would be practiced.

As a result, Celtic Christians found a way to live as something of spiritual outcasts on the British Isles. I simplify, of course. I story-tell for the sake of leading us quickly forward into time that is closer to the edge of where we stand today. But the British Isles afforded a wonderful place for there to be a strengthening and enduring of the Celtic traditions and influences, for the brand of Christianity that embraced the worship of God in all creation to flourish.

But allow me to hopscotch back to the past and offer up a name that still brings argument and causes people to become red-faced and fat-headed. It is a point of historical importance.

During the late fourth and early fifth centuries, there was a man named Pelagius, who traveled to Rome and began to speak and teach about God living in all creation. Some consider him one of the first Celtic Christians. He preached that babies were born in the image of God's goodness, not in original sin. He considered women equals who deserved to be taught how to read, learn, and discuss Scripture. Pelagius's teachings didn't go over well with the patriarchal powers, and his view of women as equals was considered a holdover from Pelagius's early life among the Celts, where the balance of feminine and masculine were recognized like the truth of the seasons: where integration and the balance of things was a focus. The weaving of him and her and us and God and all creation into one beautiful mosaic.

There are people who study Pelagius who have spent great amounts of time to either prove him right or prove him wrong. Among the writers was a spiritual director contending that Pelagius was not the heretic he was accused of being, but that his writings have been misrepresented, misinterpreted, and mistranslated. There were reports that all of his writings had disappeared, but perhaps such reports were only made to thwart anyone trying to obtain and read his writings. The truth is, many of his original writings do remain today, though most are still in the original Latin.

When it comes to Pelagius himself, I picture a Johnny Cash–type figure walking into Rome dressed in black, guitar slung across his back. Rebels in every age and time period speak out against the establishment, carrying their piece of the truth. Pelagius was that rebel for the early Celtic church, and he is a prescient voice, someone we now look to in order to understand the historical roots of the current worldwide community of interest in Celtic Christianity. In my readings of *The Letter of Pelagius to Demetrias* and other writings of his, I haven't discovered the heresies that would get him excommunicated later in life. The pope at the time wrote to encourage the bishops of Africa who opposed Pelagius to "love thy neighbor as thyself." But the encouragement came into a whole lot of political rabble-rousing at play, where favors were doled out on the side for alliances. They wanted to silence this Celtic influence. Because the history of being human and the evidence of jealousies and ambitions of power are present in every age; the story of Pelagius and his opposition all rings like current headlines.

As for his detractors, they feared and held suspect Celtic Christian traditions influenced by the pagan histories of the people. *Pagan* was used as a catch-all term, often meaning everyone who wasn't "one of us." Among the pagans, the Druids were wise men, educators, and astrologers; some call them by other names: sorcerers and wizards, the spiritual priests of the Celtic people, healers and researchers. The Druids memorized volumes of oral traditions and stories. For every bad word used to describe the influence of Druids, there was a good one that could also be applied. They held the oaks sacred along with the "wheel" of the seasons. Actual documentation about the Druids and their knowledge and beliefs was also almost entirely wiped out by the Roman Empire, and since the Druids believed that their stories, history, and knowledge all had to be maintained by oral tradition and memorization, there were few if any records written down by the Druid priests themselves. Just what amounted to volumes' worth of exquisitely memorized details of learning and creative expression.

It is understandable how the teachings of Pelagius, who celebrated all of creation—each person, animal, fish of the sea, bird of the air, tree in the forest as possessing a part of God rather than merely being created by a God who then backed away from the creation, so to speak—was considered . . . different. And *different* can so easily and so often be misunderstood.

If we had the luxury of a time machine to go back to those years, to the earliest words spoken to the Celtic people about Christ and love, about God and creation, about the Trinity as the essence of the personhood of God, we might see how the Druids, the pagans, and the rest of the Celtic tribes felt a connection to this new Christian spirituality. Perhaps it was easy for them to step over the line into Christianity. Easier than some might know because it was already alive in them, had quickened in their heart. They might have known they were reaching to embrace the very Creator whom they had been sensing nearby all those years. So they converted. But they managed to hold fast to their sense of wonder in the process.

All that was best of their Celtic nature wasn't lost in translation; they brought it to the table. Reading those histories, I think those monks of Columba's took a look at what the Celts had pulled out of their spiritual backpacks and said, "Hey, this is good. I think we can use this." So they did. And little by little, the Celtic people and Columba's missionaries blended together in ways that befitted them both and glorified God.

8

A way opens

SUDDENLY A MYRIAD OF highly unlikely details came together with the quickness of a southern streak of lightning. The kind that connected with the dirt and sent an electric hiss of a charge through the air. The kind that left a lasting impression in memory. Among the details, money arrived unexpectedly designated specifically for our plane tickets. I was overcome with a sense of wonder. God really did have a reason for this plan coming together. It was happening.

I booked our flights and was immediately thrown into the question of how we would travel once we arrived and where on earth we would stay. Having money for airline tickets was fabulous—the largest and first hurdle. But two weeks traveling in a new country without any money or hotel rooms? It sounded like something I should have ventured out on in my college years. Still, I looked out the window at the setting sun, the sky turning red on the horizon. It was all happening in perfect timing, and my perfect season was now.

I packed and repacked my backpack, trying to make everything fit, trying to lighten my load. As much as I had planned for this in my mind, I never had gotten around to that little "hike across Scotland" physical-improvement plan I'd promised myself. Our lightweight sleeping bags arrived that packed down to a pound each and attached to the outside of our backpacks. I had been slightly obsessed over these two items in the event that we stayed with hosts who had no blankets, or were stranded at a train station— or that I, as a native Floridian freezing in the November Scotland weather, might need additional layers despite a roof or blankets. Like a child with their little snuggle blanket, I needed warmth and comfort. That sleeping bag represented security, and my search to find one that would pack to nothing had been a little extreme.

As a side note on finding lodging—there are hostels that have certain age requirements. As in, they don't allow guests who are over twenty-five. This narrowed down hostel shopping choices for us a little. "Fine," I thought, "fewer options, fewer decisions." I crunched the numbers, looked at our remaining available funds, and calculated those two weeks abroad. No matter how affordable hostels might be, our budget for accommodations was roughly two dollars and fifty cents. For the entire trip.

Then I remembered something of great importance to this story. The *monastic* life of the Celtic monks. People think of monasteries as being cloistered or solitary. Of monks in their tiny cells and of the silence that must prevail in this type of life. Those portions of the business were things I could most easily comprehend and apprehend. Even the cloistered who go into the nunnery or monastery and never return. When I've had too many stressful, noisy days in a row, I think, *Sure, a cloistered, monastic life. Who doesn't want that?* But very few are actually dedicated to a cloistered lifestyle, and monastic life meant a lot more than contemplative prayer. The monastic life also was deeply dedicated to the concept of community. To being in relation with other people and serving God through serving one another. There was a way of everyone adding to the whole, making up the community so that everyone thrived by being in mission together.

This wasn't a journey where I was going to be able to travel alone as I often did, go into my hotel room alone, close the door, and enjoy those few hours of absolute solitude. My need was forcing me to embrace community. To incorporate that Celtic Christian tradition in my heart. Their understanding of the need for community and hospitality. Which brought to mind one word.

Couchsurfing.

Some eight years ago I had signed up on the website of the great social experiment known as Couchsurfing. It's like an international Airbnb, except one where people don't charge you to stay. Instead, the currency is cultural conversations. The point is to get to know people from other countries and to allow them to get to know you. In this unfolding story, I consider it an international monastic order dedicated to making friends across borders and promoting greater humanitarian efforts of understanding and compassion.

I had tried to utilize Couchsurfing years ago when I was traveling through Spain, but it had not worked out. Now, I signed on again. Updated my information. Paid to have my identification and address verified, which is an extra security measure Couchsurfing doesn't require but recommends. I had no references. In spite of this I began to reach out to different people along the way and explain I was a writer going on a pilgrimage to Iona. I made out a route, and in each city along the way where we needed to stop or catch a train, I looked for a Couchsurfing host willing to shelter two guests.

Gail from Edinburgh who loved animals wrote back that she could host us for two nights (but for only two nights). Then a man named James wrote back from Glasgow saying he could host us for two nights and that if we could wait until Saturday morning to go to Iona, he would drive us over and "wild camp" for the night. His mother used to go to the island frequently, he wrote. It was very special to her, and he would love to visit in memory of her. Okay, sure. We could change our dates around and go to Iona on Saturday.

I called Virginia and told her the good news. She pointed out that this James person could also be a serial killer. "Yes, of course," I said, "and I've already told him to expect us." Not a newbie to Couchsurfing, James was verified and had references from many people who had stayed with him previously. Our odds for survival looked really good.

Iona was getting closer. Against all odds, in spite of everything.

I carried my prayer beads in my pocket. They had become a touchstone of comfort. Something to thread my fingers through like Greek worry beads when I was trying to figure something out. Additional offers and dates from Couchsurfing hosts came back saying that we could stay with them. A PhD student would host us in Aberdeen. A young married couple would host us in a beautiful city just outside Glasgow.

The English poet, singer-songwriter, Anglican priest, and academic Malcolm Guite wrote that he could host us for a night in Cambridge, where he is currently also a Bye-Fellow and chaplain of Girton College and associate chaplain of St. Edward King and Martyr. While he often traveled, he would be in Cambridge on the night we were passing through and offered to host us as we worked our way back from Scotland and south toward London.

Then Wendy Grisham, a dear friend from the publishing industry, wrote that she would be delighted to host us in her small village south of London on our final night's stay.

From the nether of nothing, as if from the very air of lack and need, an entire world of provision and substance was forming beneath our feet. The Red Sea was parting, and we were about to travel across the ocean as if we were walking on dry land.

That's how I found myself on a cold day in November boarding a red-eye nonstop flight to the United Kingdom. This was a story made up of songlines and bread crumbs. Of a mystical island calling to me like the bells of the Roma and the possibility that orchestrating angels moved among us.

Later I would try to track all the pieces that had connected to make the trip possible. But right then, all I knew was that by the grace and providence of God, on a wing and a prayer, the stars had aligned and I was seated with my friend in the rear of British Airways Flight 222, my prayer beads in my right hand as we lifted off. We caught a tailwind over the Atlantic. In only six and a half hours we were at Heathrow Airport. London.

PART
2

ROMANCING THE ROAD

There is no road; the road is made by walking.
—ANTONIO MACHADO

Faith is a journey without maps.
—FREDERICK BUECHNER

No one regards what is before his feet; we all gaze at the stars.
—QUINTUS ENNIUS

9

we are all wanderers

When my first novel, *The Gin Girl*, was published, I went on a self-embraced book-tour wander. The publisher didn't have a budget for a book tour, and I didn't have the heart to not somehow promote the book to the best of my ability, which meant without much in the way of material means but with a lot of spirit. Until writing the novel I'd been writing with the founding members of the Loblolly Theatre Group in northwest Florida. There had been a wonderful communal spirit to pulling a show or a summer repertory together. Materials for costumes and set design came from what we often created with little or no budget. There was a wonderful comradery and sense of all for one and one for all, much like I now imagine Columba's Celtic monks experienced.

Our productions depended on everyone doing everything they could for the show to be brought to life. And theatre groups were close-knit because of this. We became a kind of monastic family rehearsing night after night until the curtain went up. There was an unquestionable sense that no matter what, regardless of position—playwright or director, actor or sound manager—we were in this thing together.

First novels are a very big deal. At least for the writer of said novel. But the experiences of opening night for a play and the publication date for *The Gin Girl* were worlds apart. With the book, it was like the curtain went up, but I found myself standing alone on stage. This was it—showtime. So I did the only thing I could think of. I got in my car and set out on the road to promote my book. I had a few dates for engagements already lined up. A book festival in a city that at that time was just a dot on the map to me—Nashville, Tennessee. And I had been invited to meet bookstore owners at the Southern Independent Bookstore Alliance. But beyond that and in between was all one grey area. So I purposed in my heart to simply turn the car in the direction I was led by gut instinct and to follow the map of my heart, like a songline. Where it called, I would follow. When I heard nothing, I'd stop. I'd figure out a way to stay somewhere as I went along. It sounded like the perfect answer. Either that or I was a bit unhinged. Either way, I made up my mind that I would do just that. And I did.

Peregrinatio Pro Christo was a practice embraced by the Celtic monks that included becoming wanderers for God. It meant becoming a person who sets out as if he or she were sailing across a great lake or ocean but without a rudder, trusting in the winds of God to guide them toward the destination.

They were wanderers for God. I was wandering to promote my book, which I know is not the same thing. But still, the girl who had longed to follow the Roma, to join them, had the wandering part down. And it gave me a first-hand experience of what it must have been like to go where the winds whispered, this way or that way. But in the way it played out, I can see how this strange idea of the Celtic people would work.

A year before the novel was published, I had been at a writing conference and met Libba, a fascinating, eclectic woman of advanced years. She had lovely spiked white hair and always only wore white head to toe. She told me that if I ever came through Charleston, South Carolina, I should come visit her in her high-rise apartment that looked out over the river. On that first wandering book tour, I rang her up and told her if the invitation to visit was still open, I'd take her up on it. She told me that we'd make it a great deal, have a party, and she gave me her address. What I discovered was that she did indeed live in a high rise by the river. It was a retirement home, and her small one-bedroom apartment looked out over the river. She lit candles when I arrived and called all her neighbors from down the hall and told them she had a famous writer staying with her and they all simply must meet me. They all came, one in a robe thrown over her pajamas, and we had coffee and cake and stayed up late telling stories around the kitchen table. The following day they took me out to lunch, to the communal dining room. A few of them bought a book from me. But more importantly, I learned something from my host who continued to invite me to stay with her, insisted that I take her bed while she slept on the sofa. Lit the candles every morning and said, "Look, the party has already started." I learned that joy of hospitality that history shows the Celtic people possessed, and that sense of true community among monastic people. Wherever I went that summer as I wandered to promote the novel, I found doors opened to me and tables set for dinner that always had room for one more. I learned that following that sense of direction that came from a place deep in my soul was sometimes the surest way to find myself right where I belonged. As I traveled the path, God showed me that, like Columba and the monks of Iona, the point was for me to live the faith, to walk it out. To embrace the path and the doing of it and at all times to walk with the understanding that I was to be a blessing to those I met as I went. To be a living epistle.

Prior to their conversion to Christianity, the Celtic tribes were wanderers as well. History doesn't offer any explanation for this other than that wandering was their M.O. They would simply pick up from one place, travel a bit, and then settle down. There appeared to be no order to the wanderings. To the person looking for clues, there were none. The travels were seemingly random, as though they flipped a coin to see if it pointed them north or decided a southward path. They did not move with the seasons or the weather or the harvest. They wandered for the joy of wandering.

The Scots have a special word for this: *stravaigin.* It means to wander about casually, to travel up and down a place. I love that there is an intersection for wandering souls found between the ancient Celts, the Celtic Christian monks, and the modern Scots. There was some sort of synergy in their wanderings and their desire to be on the move.

Like the wandering of the Roma of my childhood, the ones who called to the six-year-old girl, the ones I had dared to follow. To me, that vision of the Roma was one of meaning: living a free-spirited life filled with passion and dancing and celebration that fully embraced the mystical magic of their tradition. To me, that translates to wanderings in God, without a map.

Unlike *Peregrinatio Pro Christo*, the wandering for Christ, a pilgrimage is a specific journey to reach a site considered holy. Or a place a pilgrim feels called to. My journey to Iona fell into this category, as the birthplace of Celtic Christianity was my destination.

Truth be told, I hadn't properly considered it a pilgrimage until the plane landed in London. I had been so consumed with the timing and finances of getting there for research purposes, I had kind of looked the other way and missed the pilgrimage aspect. Pilgrimages were serious business. At least I'd always thought so. As I studied the ticket kiosk for the London subway, known locally as "the tube," a pool of silence began forming within me, a stillness. The kind of focused intent a pilgrimage requires. Virginia and I jumped on the tube, and I began thinking, yes, there were travels I had made. I'd crossed oceans, but I had never truly been on pilgrimage. I'd traveled to Europe as a happy tourist, bounced through Barcelona, caught a quick flight to Italy, ridden trains from Florence to Lucca, then to Venice and Rome. I had gone to the Vatican. And all of it had been in full-on vacation mode.

But this wasn't a vacation. And from the outset, no matter what we did or what we saw, it never felt like one. It had a purpose, and I could feel that settle on me as we arrived at our stop and climbed out into the cold sunshine of the day, which, though plentiful, couldn't warm your bones. Cold and jet-lagged, we navigated the London streets in search of our hotel while I whispered the words of Julian of Norwich, "All shall be well, and all shall be well, and all manner of thing shall be well." My pack was too heavy, and I have little bones—I am not a strong, stout woman, though I admire them. I tried not to complain about it since the packs-only rule was my idea.

We arrived before check-in and were informed our room wasn't ready. This seems to be a universal response to early guests. I would have offered to sleep on dirty sheets at that point, but rules were rules, and so we waited on the tired, old couch that was shoved in the hall toward the breakfast room, where someone stood guard at the door, protecting the kitchen cabinets from roaming hands that might raid them and load up on yogurt and granola bars. Our hotel looked suspiciously like a hostel.

When our room was finally ready, the elevator decided to break down. Right then. Perfect timing. A long line of guests were backed up waiting for it to be repaired. It occurred to me that I was indeed on a pilgrimage because pilgrims always run up against obstacles, unlike holidays that can sometimes go smooth as silk. We decided to tackle the stairs, heavy packs on our backs. I was not capable of this. I did it anyway. But it did nothing to make me feel more spiritual. Quite the opposite, as my knee hurt and my back hurt and my neck hurt.

I did not feel romantic about the ancient Celtic people. I could not remember why I even wanted to study them in the first place. I did not feel religious or in the mood for prayer. I opened the door to our box of a room. There were two tiny single beds within inches of one another in a room that would hold exactly two single beds within inches of each other. It was perfect for a couple of cloistered nuns who had taken a vow of having nothing, not even space. But it did have a small slice of a window a person could look out if they climbed up on the bed. So I did just that. I dropped my twenty-ton pack, climbed on the bed, and sat up on my knees so I could get a better view of the back of some industrial-looking buildings. It wasn't much, but anything was better than the four-foot-by-four-foot room. I propped my elbows on the tiny windowsill and looked out. My breath slowly began to sound less huffy and puffy from the stairs.

In just a little while I didn't care that our room felt like the size of a shoebox or that the window looked out over the back of old buildings instead of some lavish English garden. We were actually in London, our first stop on pilgrimage to Iona. The sun was setting, trying its best to break through a band of scattered clouds that had formed and hung so low they appeared to touch the rooftops. Just beyond the window was the grey dome of a cathedral barely visible against the backdrop of the sky that was quickly turning black. Then the last rays of sunlight latched onto the gold cross at the top of the dome. And just like that I was spiritual once again, silently whispering my thanks for safe landings and London and the road before us.

Then like the weary pilgrim that I was, with my prayer beads in my hand, I fell into a deep sleep filled with the peace of unremembered dreams.

10

THE HEARTH OF THE HEART

We woke to the dark of the London morning, the moon still high and daybreak hours away. The airport with the discount tickets to Edinburgh, Scotland, was some distance away, and the cheapest flights were also the earliest. We packed quickly and I ran through my checklist of must-haves—glasses, cell phone, charger, prayer beads. They had become a part of me now and if I had to choose any of those things to lose, the prayer beads would be the last item I was willing to give up and the easiest to let slip between the sheets and be left behind.

We checked out before the free-breakfast room was open, but the woman in charge took pity on us and made us little to-go bags of boiled eggs and scones and gave us two cups of coffee. We walked out into the frigid air where the taxi waited, motor running, headlights on. The drive would take us over forty minutes. It was the price we paid for getting such cheap airfare.

The sun creeping along the horizon gave evidence that a new day was coming, but the moon—that was a different story. She was fat and full of glory, hanging low and ripe as we crossed a bridge. We looked out across the water at the yellow of her light where she appeared to be slowly sinking beneath the surface. We were silent, all three of us—Virginia and I in the backseat, the driver—maybe each in sleepy contemplation. The taxi's tires rolled along, the blacktop threading beneath us, and it struck me that we were trusting this complete stranger to deliver us safely to our destination. What an odd thing that was. Trusting a stranger so entirely. And that in a few hours we'd be in a strange city trusting another stranger to open her door and welcome us in.

ONE OF THE MOST beautiful practices of the Celtic Christian community is that of offering warm hospitality. I consider this to be a true gift for a person to have such a welcoming heart for either friend or stranger. I have had times in my life when I was hospitable and times when I failed miserably. When I considered the possible scenarios for what hell might be like, I had a feeling I'd have one of those failed attempts replay over and over again. That I'd have to witness myself exhibiting selfish, mean, inhospitable behavior on a continuous loop.

This is the time that comes to mind. It was July 4 in Nashville, which is home to one of the largest, most extravagant fireworks displays in the entire country. Barges out in the middle of the Cumberland River in front of Nashville's Riverfront Park serve as the launchpad for an hour-long display of fireworks that boggles the mind. They explode in clusters and are exquisitely coordinated with a live performance by the Nashville Symphony. The party starts early and ends late. It brings so many visitors to the city that most hotel rooms are booked a year in advance.

One particular year I was determined that my tribe of family members would get one of the best viewing spots possible, so I went downtown hours early to secure a place for our blankets and picnic baskets. The view was prime, and I was downright proud of myself. I'm not known for being early for anything, and this had taken some serious effort. My plan was perfect and the view glorious—right until the last minute, when throngs of people arrived and began sitting and standing in every last free inch of green space, including in front of us. A large group of college-age kids all descended just as the sky lit up with the first fireworks of the night. They sat wherever they could, and many were huddled together on the grass beside us in spite of the fact that there wasn't enough room for all of them. One young girl sat down on the ground where she had been standing, which placed her firmly on the tiniest corner of my blanket. Which is when I, in rare form, told her to get off. "You are on my blanket," I kept saying. I can't imagine what made me so adamant that I couldn't share the corner of my blanket, unless I could blame it on hormones or too much caffeine. I'd be happy to find anything other than a darkness of my own human heart. And I'll never forget the hurt look in her eyes as she replied, "I'm sorry but there's just no room." Innocent, almost frightened. Someone's precious daughter.

And she was right. There hadn't been a square inch of room around us. Of all the things I've gotten wrong in life, the places where I made the wrong decision, this is the moment that haunts me and feels as if it was the greatest sin I've ever committed—not being willing to share the tiniest corner of what was mine. Not a smidge. Basically acting like the bitch I am not, but was that night and never want to be again.

I have seen what true hospitality looks like. You'd think having witnessed what that looks like and being a recipient of someone's grace, I'd be better at emulating that example.

Some years ago I traveled with a group of women to a conference in Orlando. We had money for the basics—fuel and food—but not for hotel rooms for seven women. Carmen, a friend of one of the women in the group, told her we were welcome to stay with her. We were delighted to have a place to stay. All seven of us.

When we arrived at her apartment building, Carmen was outside waiting for us as we pulled into the parking lot. She clapped her hands with excitement, which was accompanied by a steady stream of Spanish welcomes in many words, some of which I understood, and the rest spoken so fast that I couldn't keep up. After giving each of us a hug, she grabbed someone's suitcase and signaled for us to follow her. Carmen explained that her young daughter would sleep with her so that someone could sleep in her bed, and then she opened the door to her daughter's room with a grand sweep of her hand. Four extra mattresses were spread across the floor, along with one box spring. These had all come from neighbors who offered to share what they had when she told them about our upcoming visit. The accommodations were presented to us as if we had stepped into a luxury penthouse suite, and Carmen's sincere welcome made me feel exactly like there could be no finer arrangements ever made.

Later, with the same enthusiasm, she offered us steaming plates of black beans and rice. "It may be simple, yes," she said, "but we are blessed, and I am so happy to have so many new sisters around my table." This was all in Spanish, but I understood this much. Sometime during this dinner she was told I wasn't Spanish and most likely couldn't understand most of what she was saying. Then Carmen said to me, in English, "You look Spanish, yes? You know this? I thought you were Spanish." I have never felt more welcomed in my life, and that experience served as an example of what true hospitality really was. That it wasn't about my surroundings or material abundance. It wasn't about whether my walls needed a new coat of paint or that my fixer-upper was in a constant state of needing a lot more fix and a truckload of up. It was my *heart* that mattered, the spirit in which I offered whatever I had, regardless of how simple.

Welcoming stranger or friend with an open heart and an open door. This too was the trait of the ancient Celtic people. They would have considered Carmen one of their own. They might have put me in time-out.

For the ancient Celtic people, it was the holy act of sharing that mattered. It was offering the bread and cup of relationship. Of equal importance, and not to be overlooked, was being a good receiver, accepting gifts and hospitality with grace and thankfulness. And it was in that spirit that I had gratefully slept on the box spring at Carmen's home.

When I first thought of Couchsurfing and considered it a viable alternative to hotels or hostels, it was mostly due to lack of funds. What I soon discovered was that hospitality was a key component of the Celtic spirit. And God used that to further us on our journey. Little by little this pilgrim was making progress within and without.

An elderly woman had told my fortune once, quite unbidden and unexpected, when I was visiting a rather large book club in Atlanta. She had been eating M&M's at the time—one of those odd things one remembers for no reason at all—when she leaned in toward me and whispered, "You will trust yourself in strange places." I laughed at the time. She had taken me so by surprise and it had nothing to do with the upcoming discussion about my novel. But odd as it was, I have always remembered it. And now, I was in a place I didn't find strange, but it was a strange place in that it was new. And I did indeed trust myself. To find a way to go and people to connect with and, should anything go awry—I trusted the situation would be made straight again.

After catching our early flight on a budget airline from London and landing in Edinburgh, we huddled out of the rain in a bar for a bit and chatted with the people who worked there, where we just wanted to eat up that Scottish accent with a spoon. Then we stepped out and got in the queue for a taxi, gave the driver Gail's address, and he said something about a very nice place by the park. In only twelve minutes he pulled up into a neighborhood of stately townhomes that didn't look like anything I had imagined a Couchsurfing host living in. I expected something a bit more casual.

Gail opened her door to us in her four-story walk-up that lay but a stone's throw from the oldest pub in Scotland, the Sheep Heid Inn. Our host had red hair, that lovely accent, and two new rescue dogs. She had dinner ready for us and offered us a cup of tea as she set the table.

I thought, *This is what trusting yourself can look like. This is what trusting strangers can be like. This is what the entire world could look like on any given day if we decided to just sit down and have a cup of tea and get to know one another.*

Our room was on the fourth floor of her townhome, and all prepared for our arrival. We stored our things upstairs, amazed at the beautiful surroundings and at how this person had opened her home to us, trusting that we were not serial killers. Unlike Gail and James, we had no references.

Over dinner, we shared stories about our journey, explaining that I was on a quest, on a pilgrimage, and writing a book about my travels. She asked about where we lived and how far it was from Texas, where she had lived for three years. She missed the bright skies and the people.

Gail was a fiery person, passionate in that way that makes some people seem so alive. She'd joined Couchsurfing so that she could meet people from around the world. When she'd lived in Texas, she had quite loved it. "All that sunshine!" But as much as she loved those years, her passion for Scotland, its history, and its future ran deep in her veins.

She was also a Reiki practitioner and believed strongly in spiritual energies. So had the Celts. So did I. She spoke to us of the full moon and how we might call things to us that we wanted when the new moon was in the sky, or decide what we might want to let go of as the moon turned to full and began waning. That was time, she said, to let things go.

I was a moon girl. I felt its power when it was full. All of nature seems to respond to the moon as well. The coyotes always howl up on my hill. And often, the moon wakes me so that I wander outside on my porch, watch the way the light filters through the trees or how it lights up the empty field across the way. In a pitch-dark room I feel the moon pull me awake like the tides. So when Gail spoke of the moon, of spiritual energies and the healing power of Reiki, I didn't discount her words. This, too, was a part of the Celtic nature. They knew about energies, about the power of God in all creation, that something that could control the tides of the earth could also surely affect the human heart.

On that night the moon called to me as was her usual. I quietly walked down the four flights of stairs from our bedroom. I made hot tea, opened the door to the patio, and stepped outside. A field much like those that neighbor my property back home lay just beyond the fence, and the full moon in her hospitable glory cast such light that I could have recognized a friend from a great distance.

It was November in Edinburgh, and the trees were bare and the air cold. Like a view through a tightly focused lens, I saw a crispness to it all. Each branch stood out against the light, declaring itself a living sketch of art. In spite of my coat and the hot tea, I was no match for the temperature, and begged the moon with apology to release me and let me go back to my bed, where I snuggled under the down comforters and felt like an honored guest of a Scottish goddess.

I imagined Columba's monks wandering those ancient hills, wandering in the light of that same old moon, wandering into the settlements of Celtic tribes and being offered their hospitality for the night. The sharing of bread and drink. And the monks receiving gladly and offering what they had to offer, news of this Christ.

11

THE WORLD OF LIGHT AND SHADOW

THEY BELIEVED IN ANGELS and they believed in demons. In the forces of good and the shadows of evil. They were superstitious and they were believers. They prayed St. Patrick's words, "Christ in peace, Christ in danger," and they prayed for the encircling of protection, as if they were weaving a spell of light, of God. Three being the magic number and as part of their prayers for protection from evil, they would sometimes make the rounds, walk three times around a cross, a home, or a person, encircling them with the good and sealing the evil out.

The Celtic people had long understood that both darkness and light were part of their lives. And they understood the space O'Donohue referred to as the "Celtic consciousness being a penumbral light," which belonged neither to the light nor to the dark. They were aware of the space in between. What they would call the threshold and the thin places, which we'll speak of now and later. They knew the pause as night becomes morning and day becomes night again. The space of thresholds and thin places. Doorways to different dimensions or times. The crossing of one to another as thin as a dime, a hair, a hope.

The imaginary Callanish Stones of the Outlander book series by Diana Gabaldon are an example of what some would consider a thin place; in her fictional stories, they held the possibility of traveling through time and between physical locations.

There are also holy sites around the world considered thin places. Lori Erickson in her book *Holy Rover* describes why she holds to the Celtic concept of thin places, and how she found Machu Picchu to be just that. I've experienced what seemed to be a thin place in time, where time itself took on a different quality. And I've experienced a thin place that made heaven feel one breath, one step away, and good. I've also stood in a thin place where I just wanted to get gone as fast as a bat out of hell before something straight out of Hades grabbed me and pulled me in and ate me.

Our guide and host, whom we affectionally called Goddess Gail, decided to drive us to the train station, but she was determined to take us to see Rosslyn Chapel before we left. Which I found a little odd since it was an hour in the opposite direction (which took me an hour farther away from Iona). But we gladly accepted an opportunity to see firsthand this place that had caused such a stir and drew millions of visitors. I was a true chapel girl in that I loved them and was up for a chapel tour in any city. I knew that the Rosslyn Chapel had been made quite famous by the Dan Brown book *The Da Vinci Code* and Tom Hanks's portrayal of the lead character in the movie series. And that was all I knew. Officially known as St. Matthew's–Rosslyn Chapel, it is small inside, in the way of most chapels. Chapels are dear to me because I find them intimate, and they make God feel more accessible in the same way the practices of Celtic Christianity do. As we moved through the space, I began to notice the details of the stone carving in the chapel. Scrollwork, leaves, trees, animals, and carvings of what was called "The Green Man." And *more* carvings of The Green Man, and yet more carvings of . . . The Green Man. There were over one hundred carvings featuring The Green Man. I almost laughed aloud during the tour. Most people believed that The Green Man had originated with the ancient Celts and Druids and symbolized life and renewal. A pre-Christian symbol or entity, he was associated with the earth, and also with the spirit of the ending of seasons or of death. Renewal, death, rebirth.

I was sitting in a Christian chapel with a hundred stone images of the ancient spirit or entity of The Green Man, and also rumored to secretly house the Holy Grail, the cup of Christ. It was a place cloaked in mystery of every sort. Dark and light. The stone staircase of an apprentice murdered out of jealousy by the master. Hidden musical notes said to create a masterpiece. Riddles and clues in the carvings. A portal for time travel, a hiding place for the mummified head of Christ. All of this right before me as I sat in the beautiful, quiet chapel with candles flickering and light streaming in through the windows. It was as if all the mysteries intersected at this point. The old gods and the new and in the center, the threshold of the thin place whose door opened both to life and to death. Perhaps it was up to the visitor to choose.

12

THE Progression
OF Pagans

As we stepped off the train in the city of Glasgow, I felt an instant sense of belonging. Two seconds off the train, Virginia and I both declared, "I love it here!"

A street performer was singing as we found our way through the streets and hailed a cab, giving him our new temporary address.

Duncan, the taxi driver, was a storyteller who almost drove looking backwards at us as he tried to share about his annual pilgrimage to the States to a place called Las Vegas where he won enough money last year to pay for his trip. It was one story after the other until he found our address, and we said good night, realizing as he drove away that we didn't know where we were, if we were on the right street or even in the right neighborhood. At that moment, James opened his door, and light poured out onto the sidewalk.

We followed his lilting voice up the stairs to his flat and, once inside, were overcome by the expansive view from his window out over the lights of Glasgow. We were awestruck by the presence of this stranger who offered us his home and asked nothing of us in return but stories of who we were and where we were from.

Over cups of tea we talked about the Isle of Iona, and he told us of his mother, who had passed away when he was just sixteen. She had worked for the church and had often gone to Iona, and it had been her favorite place. He told us again why he was willing to drive us, that it was in memory of her. To pay his respects to her that way. So we made our plan.

James let us know he was a psychiatrist, something that hadn't been listed on his Couchsurfing profile. He said he'd be off to the office first thing and be gone for the day. We made plans to meet for dinner when he returned.

I counted down the hours to Iona. Pilgrimages are never an easy and immediate sort of business. You cannot just get on a plane in Nashville because you are going to Atlanta on pilgrimage, or take a direct flight to London, step off the plane, and say, "There, I did it. Mission accomplished." Pilgrimages require determination, desire, dedication, time. A kind of holy perseverance. They also often require the odd occurrence, the help from a stranger, the kindness of a friend. This pilgrimage of mine required all of that.

The following day we visited the Kelvingrove Art Gallery and Museum and threaded our way through the exhibits to find a huge statue of Elvis in blue. We had come all the way from Tennessee to find Elvis in Glasgow. Which just proved he never left the building.

Upstairs I found the Salvador Dali painting *Christ of St. John of the Cross*. I'd never seen anything like it. No one had until Dali saw it within himself, captured it, and painted it. The crucifixion was painted from an entirely different perspective: from above the cross, with a view of Christ on the cross and the world below. In the distance is a small fishing boat at rest, the suggestion of a dove, of resurrection, a calmness that defied the moment or looked beyond it.

Salvador Dali wanted to be the first artist to paint images that combined science and religious belief. For a time he gave up his Catholicism, but later in life he requested an audience with the pope. He studied nuclear physics and felt that the discovery of the atomic nature of the universe proved the existence of God. As he pursued scientific studies and religion within an arts frame, he called this art *nuclear mysticism* and went so far as to print his mystical manifesto announcing his intention. Pope Pius XII gave Dali approval for his religious themes. Either God had been with him or Salvador Dali was extremely persuasive, or a bit of both.

Looking at the painting, I understood the desire and passion to communicate that God and the field of physics were interwoven. Like Dali, I believed the discoveries of science pointed ever more strongly to the evidence of God. In a recent conversation with astrophysicist Paul Wallace, I shared with him my idea about how science unlocks the wonders of God: that each discovery is like opening a box, and inside that box, you actually find a larger box that contains a larger box, into infinity. The idea being that each new discovery simply unlocks the reality of a greater truth of God in all creation. It widens our understanding of the universe and, with it, the nature and the existence of Dali's great mystical Creator.

I walked slowly from painting to painting until I came to another large canvas, captivating me the way that art does by communicating everything at once. In front of me was a collaboration titled *The Progression of the Pagans*, in which the artists captured a series of priests from different cultures and times in history. Each of the subjects was respectfully presented as they all turned their eyes toward the eastern horizon. Each was regal in dress and stature. A sea of holy men and women searching for and believing in something greater than they were.

The companion piece that hung next to it was titled *The Annunciation*, and an angel of God appeared to the shepherds as they watched over their flocks, to announce the birth of Christ. I thought of the Celtic tribes in all their splendor and of Columba arriving, announcing the birth of Christ to them, and sharing his story.

It was the same story told again. And at once I was among the pagans looking to the horizon, searching for the Spirit, sensing the holiness of existence and the magic of other dimensions. And I was the shepherds in the field guarding the flocks, keeping watch, standing between them and the dangers of the night, blinded by the sudden light of heaven. And I was the angel saying, "Look. Don't be afraid. A savior is born."

And I was the Celtic people wandering the coast, roaming free and at random with exalted abandon, blessing the fire, watching the moon, dancing in celebration of all of creation.

And I was Columba, in self-imposed exile, determined and penitent, rocking in a boat out on the seas, searching for the outermost end of the earth and the threshold at heaven's door.

13

THEN THERE
WERE THREE

LATER THAT EVENING, WE walked with James down the street from his flat to the Stravaigin restaurant, where they proudly advertised that they had been "wandering since 1994," and that they were offering up "glad tidings of comfort, food and joy." A little travelers' paradise. It was also a dog-friendly establishment, so we made fast friends with a furry beast who lodged himself under our table, refusing to return to his owner for the rest of the evening, possibly influenced by the fries I'd been slipping him out of sight.

Back at James's place later that night, a new friend of his stopped by to invite him to her graduation at Aberdeen

University, even though they'd met only a few months before. Hospitality continued to be part of each interaction. Where strangers were no longer strangers. I loved the late meeting with Neisa and promised to stay in touch even as I begged off to bed and said my goodnights like I'd lived there forever.

The following morning, the weather was with us. The forecast was for mostly sunshine, and so James, Virginia, and I packed up a picnic and headed for the only road from Glasgow that runs up the west coast, trundling past Loch Lomond and towns named Crianlarich, Tyndrum, and Bridge of Orchy. Between Tyndrum and Bridge of Orchy lies the West Highland Way, a ninety-six-mile footpath parallel to the road, with people trekking along as we sped past, trying to reach the last ferry of the day. The hill that opens up at the top of the pass is called Beinn Dorain, which means "the hill of the otter," and we drove through Glencoe, with the majestic pyramidal Buachaille Etive Mor mountain on our left.

Our plans were to catch the Corran Ferry, which navigates the Corran Narrows of Loch Linnhe just south of Fort William and north of the Ballachulish Bridge. Then we would drive to Lochaline and take another ferry to Fishnish, and then on to the Isle of Mull, where we were to spend the night. We would stay at a small bed-and-breakfast there, owned by a family of sheepherders, and take the ferry to Iona early the following morning.

Along the way, we talked about molecular DNA and inherited memory, how story literally runs through our veins from generation to generation. Virginia mentioned that since we were going on this quest and the road had been so long, it was like we were in *The Wizard of Oz* and I was Dorothy and she was the scarecrow. Then she asked James which character he was. He replied, "I'm the red shoes."

Indeed. Red shoes. The magical carpet, the wagon and bells, the way that we moved.

We made the Corran Ferry in time to be the first car on, and we were proud of ourselves after our late start that we had arrived right on schedule. It wasn't until we were blocked in by all the other cars that pulled in behind us that we learned that the Lochaline-to-Fishnish ferry was not operating because the slipway was being re-concreted. This meant we had to actually depart from the ferry, drive down the road, turn around, and board the same ferry again before it left that dock to return.

James apologized profusely for the delay, although it was no fault of his. He searched for any possibilities of alternate routes. We called the owner of the house where we planned to stay on Mull. With some concern she said we'd have to go to Oban to catch the late ferry there. It was our only hope. Somewhere in the quickening dark, over the islands and lochs, beyond the sheep and the long-haired cattle, or *Heilan coo*, in the fields, Iona was silently waiting.

Backward was our only way forward.

Again, we were the first car on board the ferry, only this time we were headed in the opposite direction. We returned to our starting point, then wound our way around to the city of Oban, almost an hour away, to catch the last ferry to Mull. That's when the warning light came on telling James that his very fine Skoda—much like an Audi, a great touring vehicle for those who love to drive—had a tire that was fast losing air.

LET US SPEAK OF the number three.

When I was eight years old, we had left Germany and were once again living in the States, and were visiting my grandmother. My mother and father were taking her out to the dog races. At the time people weren't aware of the negative issues related to dog racing, and now I have many friends who have adopted greyhounds from rescue organizations because they make wonderful family pets. This was a time people were also smoking cigarettes without realizing any of the harmful side effects. My grandmother didn't drive and she didn't get out much, and the dog races were the closest place to take her to try to offer her a little excitement. It was an evening she'd been looking forward to. Feeling guilty for leaving me behind with my aunt for the evening, my mother asked me if I'd like her to place a bet for me. I told her to please bet on the third dog in the third race to come in third. I obviously had an affection for the number three at a young age. It hasn't waned. Later that night my mother came in and let me know that I had won three dollars.

The Celtic people are also more than a little fond of the number three and consider it sacred. The triquetra, a symbol made of three interlaced arcs and a circle, was adopted by the Celtic Christians to denote the Trinity. The triskele, a triple spiral, is another sign that utilizes the power of three, and the circular manner in which it is drawn immediately brings the ancient Celtic people to mind. The oldest such symbol discovered by archaeologists is over five thousand years old and was found in the Newgrange passageway located in the Boyne Valley of Ireland.

If you had a transparency of the things Christianity introduced and you laid it over the things the Celtic people believed and held sacred, you would discover a lot of overlap, and even places that fit together perfectly. The number three is one of those things. The Celtic people already held the number three in reverence, so when monks approached them speaking of a triune God made up of the Father, Christ, and the Holy Spirit, it is not surprising that they easily accepted this Christian God. It is equally understandable that the Irish monks, separated by wars and distance from the Roman church, could so appreciate the God of creation that they shared the sensibilities of the Celts. They approached one another already speaking the same spiritual language.

Part of this shared language is the recognition of the power of the three and the way it can be embraced and utilized. Whereas I had been alone in my quest to search for meaning in the Celtic Christian path, I had been joined by Virginia, whom O'Donohue would certainly consider an *anam cara* to me, a soul friend for the journey. Although the two of us had gotten as far as we could together, James now made three.

A three-braided rope is exponentially stronger than a strand of two. In spite of the difficulties and obstacles that lay ahead, as three we would be stronger in the overcoming. And while I had always held to the importance of three, now we all began to see three as a magic number.

14

PILGRIMS IN OBAN

JAMES DROVE TO OBAN as fast as he dared, and we arrived at the city and reached the water in time to discover that it would still be two hours before we could buy a ticket on the ferry and line up our car on the dock. The bridge didn't open until eight, but it closed soon after, so the timing called for travelers to buy a ticket and then sit and wait for two hours for the ferry to arrive.

In the meantime, James's tire was still signaling that it was losing air. But we remained light-hearted with expectations that all would work out well. No one became testy or angry. No one had known that the ferry routes could change or be stopped completely. Why would a ferry be closed? That never happened. And our attitude on the way to Oban had been as cheerful as it had been earlier along the way. We were taking our obstacles in stride, and I, for one, knew that no pilgrimage was without obstacles.

Obstacles are just part of the process. I wish I could remember this for a multitude of things life throws my way on any given day. That I could apply it on days when troubles seem like flies I have to swat down left and right.

When I pulled back and looked at the preparation for this journey from the long view, I could see it was *all* one long pilgrimage to the holy land with, thankfully, times just for sitting in silence or for wandering without intent. There were actually times to live without deadlines and treasured moments on my porch on the hill.

I could change the rhythm of my days. They could follow a more monastic way of life. I could incorporate the lessons learned on my Iona journey and the Celtic Christian disciplines I had discovered into my daily living and weave them into a new way of life. Otherwise, what was all the worry and fuss to get here? God didn't just intend for me to merely write a few words. God intended for the writing of the words to change me.

James parked the car, and Virginia noticed that there was a parking meter and put change in so we wouldn't get a ticket. I found a bookstore, and we wandered and perused until we decided a meal would be in good order. I loved what I noticed as a natural ebb and flow of conversation, of the way Virginia and I had taken turns riding in the backseat without any discussion, just changing at odd stops along the way. I loved the way that we separated and wandered different aisles in the store and how, without any conversation, we all came together again at the front of the store and crossed the street to the restaurant for fish and chips. Naturally! If you ever go to the UK or to Scotland, people will tell you in every city and every pub that you must get the fish and chips. You can get them anywhere, but I recommend that you drive out of your way to go to Oban, where you can choose from three different types of fresh fish. And you can order a scotch named Oban 14 made in the town.

James hadn't eaten fish and chips for three years because he is fit as a fiddle and when he is not at his day job being a psychiatrist, he does strange things like biking across the Andes and Himalayas. But tonight, we were overcoming obstacles and caught in the furnace of our trials. If such a crucible isn't a time to indulge, well, perhaps at least this once he decided it stood to reason as he was stranded in a city with two strange women on a pilgrimage that he hadn't planned.

James doesn't appear to be what one would call a "religious" person, but he does seem to follow his spiritual instincts where they whisper and lead. He told us that when he received my Couchsurfing request, although he is a psychiatrist who prides himself on scientific understanding of the workings of the mind, he checked in with his "gut instinct" before saying yes to me. And when I told him I was on pilgrimage to Iona, he knew it was meant to be.

Now, out of the blue, James offered, "How strange to be here. My ex-wife and I came here to get married. A small, quiet affair in this little city." He texted her, "I'm in Oban. Happy anniversary." For the longest time they had not been on speaking terms, but recently, that had changed. She had invited him for Christmas dinner. Time and age heal some things. She texted him back, "LOL." All was indeed well on that cold Oban night. We ate fish and drank scotch by candlelight.

We paid our bill and traveled back to the docks, and the freezing cold was all the station had to offer. We tried all the doors, but it wasn't yet open. I asked the four ferry attendants questions. They were huddled in the ferry ticket booth, and when they answered me each time, their accents were so heavy and so happy and they were trying to help so much, but I didn't understand a word they were saying. And I just kept repeating, "What does that mean?" And they laughed. And I laughed in this place where we had found ourselves quite by accident and were not meant to be at all.

James tried to change the tire that had gone flat, and told Virginia and me to please stay inside the car as the wind that came across the water whipped at us and was biting. Our teeth were chattering, so we took him up on the offer. Even though we felt a bit guilty, we stayed inside and remained a slight shade warmer.

Trouble, trouble, boil and bubble. He tried to remove the tire, but it wouldn't budge. Then we heard another voice, a man who had ambled along from somewhere and stopped to help. I didn't know how much help he would be; he was a clam diver who had been drinking down a few to try to digest the news that the captain of his boat had determined that, despite this cold weather and such rough seas, they would still be going out the following day. He had three children, he said, and no choice but to keep his job. His paycheck. His livelihood. We found this news out later from James when the tire had been replaced with the spare. James thanked him for stopping, and Leon had replied, "I never fucking wouldn't stop," in that great accent of a Scot who worked the ocean all winter long. A rough-and-tumble kind of guy who could take it as it came but was intent on always being a better man. James responded that he hoped that worked well the other way, that people stopped for him as well. Leon replied, "Sometimes they do; sometimes they don't. But I don't judge, man. I don't judge nobody for nothing."

Leon was a light in the darkness. We all said, "God bless Leon." Now I say it most days. When I share his story with other people, they also say, "God bless Leon." This counts for something. I know it does. Sometimes we entertain angels unaware. Sometimes we are completely unaware that we have become the angels.

The ferry was almost empty and extremely cold. Except for the bar, which we found our way to quickly and ordered Guinness. The bartender's name was Brian. He had a great tattoo of a crucifix on his beefy forearm. I told him I liked it, and I told him about Dali's *Christ of St. John of the Cross*. He said he had heard about it and he'd love to see it someday. Then we chatted a little about some simple things. He was a big man with tired, kind eyes, and I hoped the long night ahead of him would pass well.

It was so late my brain had a hard time processing the events of the day. Slowly I unlatched my backpack, then let it fall to the floor, knowing it would be a job to stand back up and get it on. The spirit was willing but the body was all kinds of weary. I plopped down on the floor beside it, sat cross-legged, leaning my back against that pack that was supposed to weigh a mere twenty-something pounds. It felt like a rock, and with every mile we had traveled and with every passing hour as the night came on, it had grown heavier by degrees. I marveled that we had actually traveled all that way from Glasgow, made it to the edge of Scotland, boarded a ferry so that we could board another ferry, but then had to turn around, board the same ferry back to race up through that falling darkness so we could catch the last-chance ferry. In spite of all of it I was satisfied, knowing that as the ferry now churned the dark, cold waters at her bow, I was closing the distance to Iona, answering the call like those Roma bells from so long ago. Except this time, I had the freedom to follow.

And before much longer they announced it was time for passengers to return to their cars and to disembark on the Isle of Mull. I shoved my prayer beads back in my pocket and managed to get the pack up on my back one more time.

15

THE ISLE OF MULL

W E STILL HAD AN hour's drive through the dark to get to the bed-and-breakfast. The innkeeper's directions included something about passing sheep on the right, and that there would be a sign that said to turn left but that we were *not* to turn there but to continue down the road until we saw a gate. James seemed a little concerned about the loosey-goosey directions filled with descriptions of sheep and gates and approximates. He was tired, it was dark, and he wanted exacts and specifics.

I was sitting in the back this time, quietly keeping my eyes on the landscape that was barely lit by the headlights. I had pulled my prayer beads out, and I ran my fingers over them as we drove down the small one-way road. It was indeed an island, not a city, and there were no streetlamps to light the night. No blur of city lights miles off in the distance. No porch lights of houses dotting the way. Wherever we were, we were, for all purposes, together. The three of us. Three, that magical number.

THE ISLE OF MULL has nothing but narrow lanes called one-ways because they only allow one car to go one way at a time. If another car approaches from the opposite direction, someone must decide to pull over to allow the other car to pass. I remember no other cars that night. Just us moving forward into the darkness, James's headlights the only light at all, our world consisting of those orbs of light and the distance they could reach. Nothing beyond them, and the absolute absence of things, and my thinking, "This place is beautiful, truly beautiful." And I knew when I woke up, I'd see with my eyes what my heart already suspected.

We passed the sheep, then the sign that said "Turn Here," where we weren't supposed to turn, and traveled farther until we arrived at a house with a porch light on. That had to be the place. *Finally, a warm place and a warm bed.*

Only, we discovered, it wasn't so warm. The heat turned off at ten o'clock, and it was after midnight, and the cold had seeped its way into every corner, every stone, and all my bones. I kept wandering through the house searching for buttons, dials, knobs, directions, propane—anything I could twist or turn or strike a match to that would bring a hiss and a kiss of a flame and the sudden warmth of heat.

James took pity on me and lent me his beautiful "jumper," which turned out to be a sweater, not a romper suit. I wanted to steal it, but that wouldn't bode well or bring good karma for a pilgrimage. I huddled in wool and blankets.

Virginia opened wine and found muffins that had been left over from breakfast, and James asked if he could visit us in our room. He propped up on one bed and Virginia on the other while I sat cross-legged on the floor, and we told stories like pilgrims around a campfire with all the pent-up, worn-out energy of children who have gone way too long past their bedtime. We were electrified with the trying and the doing and the overcoming. And tomorrow, come hell or high water, we would get to Iona.

PART 3

A SUNDAY KIND OF HOPE

Hope is a waking dream.

—ARISTOTLE

The light in the Celtic consciousness is a penumbral light.

—JOHN O'DONOHUE

Truths kindle light for truths.

—LUCRETIUS

16

SAVED BY THE EGG BOY

I WOKE EARLY, FOUND INSTANT coffee, and grabbed a cup before I zipped up a coat and stepped out into the morning on Mull. I had slept in my clothes, inside my sleeping bag, under two down comforters. If I had found more blankets, I would have used them. But now there was the slightly warming heat from the morning sun. A low, cloudy haze hung over the ridge that faced us, but it appeared once again that the weather was with us. I knew that on an island, that could change with short notice or none at all.

With coffee in hand, I opened the front gate and stepped out into the road. The innkeeper's sheep stood by the fence, watching me intently. They were solid white with the exception of their black faces, and I thought them the finest sheep I'd ever seen. Scattered along up the hill as far as I could see, they stood out, brilliant against the green of Scotland. I walked down the road, reveling in the feel of the dirt of Scotland under my boots. I was a world away from my hill in Tennessee. I was a pilgrim in a strange land that felt oddly familiar.

I returned just in time to meet the innkeeper's mother, who was serving us a "large Scottish breakfast," a crazy amount of food that I supposed was meant to sustain us for a good trek up into the hills. I thought it enough to survive for a month should we be trapped by a rockslide. There were sausages and eggs and blood pudding and potatoes. Virginia asked Gillian what was in the blood pudding, and the secret ingredient to all that goodness was in its name: blood. Wanting to honor the Celtic hospitality I had studied and experienced, I took a bite to be a gracious guest and smiled at the host. "'Tis tasty," I said and reached for my coffee.

I did have one small request.

"Do you think we could light a fire there in the hearth?"

"Oh, just come out and help me with the sheep," she said. "That'll warm you up. I've been out there since four in the morning working them, and I've got a good sweat still."

Working the sheep wasn't exactly on my agenda for the day. (Note to self for future travels: Pack foot warmers, and hand warmers, and firewood.)

Gillian then explained how you could tell the weather by looking across the fields to the cliff headland, or "Burg," that rose there. The lovely Scottish accent once again presented me with a challenge. It was difficult to understand the words, but they were delivered with such enthusiasm by everyone I met that I was always reluctant to ask anyone in Scotland to repeat themselves. But for the most part, we understood that Gillian was referring to the name of the cliff, and that you could tell if the ferries would be running that day based on how the water flowed across its face.

Burg was on the Ardmeanach Peninsula. *Ardmeanach* means "middle promontory" in Gaelic. Gillian explained that when the lovely waterfall that cascades into the waves of the Atlantic Ocean on the western side of the island is obscured from view, it means it is raining heavily. She also added that when the waterfall appears to turn back upon itself due to heavy westerly winds, then it means it is unlikely that the boats can land on Staffa, one of the islands, and possibly not on Iona either.

This I understood completely: If the waterfall turned back on itself, then the ferry to Iona couldn't run. Then she told us a bit of other news: The Iona ferry didn't run this time of year unless it had been pre-booked by someone. We fell silent.

During the spring and summer months the ferry ran an all-day schedule. But this was November. The little shops and restaurants were closed. No one was there, so the ferry had no reason to run. That was, unless someone scheduled a trip in advance. Then the ferry would stop by Mull and pick them up and take them to Iona.

"The best thing you can do," offered Gillian, the stout and steady, warm sheepherding innkeeper, "is just drive to the ferry dock and hope someone has reserved it, and if they have, you can buy a ticket and get on."

Virginia and I left the majority of our big breakfasts on our plates as we rushed to pack. Gillian's mother returned for the dishes and said, "Oh, they don't eat? Why don't they eat? Don't they like it?" But when she saw James's plate, we were absolved. He had eaten every last bite like a good Scottish boy.

Once back in the car, everything loaded, James apologized again for the ferry business. For not knowing ahead of time about what ferries were shut down or the fact that one had to make reservations for the Iona ferry. I assured him not to worry. It wasn't his fault. And I hadn't come this far just so that I could stand on the Isle of Mull and look across the water at the Isle of Iona and turn and go home.

"If we have to, we'll find a fisherman in a boat to row us across."

"I don't know; there may not be anyone like that," James said with a worried tone. His concern that we'd come so far and might not get to the island weighed on him. He was dedicated to this pilgrimage now. He had to see it through.

"I promise you," I said, "we will find someone with a boat if we have to. We will get across." I meant this with all of my being.

We drove down the one-way, slowly dodging the sheep that appeared to be catching the same ferry. They led the way, their coats full and each of them marked with a bit of pink or blue on their wool to designate whose sheep was whose. We arrived at the ferry office and discovered we were more than a little fortunate. The ferry hadn't stopped lately, but someone had booked it for that day—a grandmother going to see her daughter and grandson who lived on Iona. It was surprising that such a small island had year-round residents. But then, it had been the site of an active monastery where, over the years, so many monks and nuns had lived out their entire lives in community. It had been the birthplace of Celtic Christianity, which had spread throughout Britain and beyond, eventually finding its way across the Atlantic to the city of Nashville.

The grandmother arrived, and we thanked her profusely for visiting her grandson. "Without you, we would have been stranded," James said.

"You saved us," I told her. Although I meant it, I still carried my private belief: *But if not for you, we would have found a boat.* I looked out at the water. We were going to cross, no matter what. God would have made a way, even if it had been by hot air balloon.

Until the ferry arrived, we scouted the beach, turned over rocks and shells, took pictures of birds and waves and sky. Now that we had done everything—crossed the ocean and the United Kingdom and made new friends and driven

up the coast, taken three ferries and driven the one-ways—
it had come down to nothing to do but wait.

The Isle of Mull seemed a charming place, a place where
I could write and walk the beach and count the blue sheep
and the pink sheep at night before I fell asleep. I could stay
here on writing sabbatical, I thought. The island invited you
that way. Into its community to be alone. Gillian had said
no one on Mull ever locked their doors. Not one of them.
That if someone came in your house, it would be a friend
who needed you or was checking to see if you needed anything. Why make them knock? I could live in a land like
that, learn to not lock my door. In due time, of course.

Finally, the ferry arrived, and we walked onto the small
boat. I planted my face at the window, watching Iona grow
larger as we drew nearer to her shore.

The grandmother began to brag about her grandson
the way that grandmothers have license to do. "He's the egg
boy of Iona," she said.

"The egg boy?" I asked.

"Oh yes, he has the finest chickens, and he takes care
of them, and he sells their fresh eggs every day. He comes
down to the dock and meets the ferry with his eggs. That's
why they call him the egg boy of Iona."

So that was who we had to thank. After all we'd been
through, every part of the journey, all the twists and turns
and the fine accommodations, it came down to a child,
an innocent, who made it finally possible. Or was it the
chickens who laid the eggs that the boy sold? Or was it the

multitudes who had lived and died on Iona long before the egg boy was ever born? Yes, as the Celtic people would recognize, there wasn't one thing that was separate from another. And we were all part of the wheel that turned from one season to another, one life to another, and it took all of us to make up the whole.

The ferry docked at Iona, and the bridge was lowered for us to walk ashore. I had arrived.

17

Revelation in the Ruins

There is always something that affects me when I walk through sites where there are remnants of a society that has come and gone. The skeletal remains of entire communities echoing from the stones they left behind. The ghost cities of the Anasazi carved within the rocks of the Southwest United States. The paintings found on the walls of the caves of Borneo and in Indonesia. The ruins of a monastery with stones still standing.

Somewhere here a man built a fire; somewhere there a woman stirred a pot; in this corner of the cave a baby nestled at his mother's breast. I reach to touch this thread of life that carried us forward, vow to not let go. We belonged to the people who came before us, and we belong to them still. And they remind me that I have to be about the business of my life, which is to live it fully, without apology and without regret.

This is what the ruins spoke to me on Iona as I slowly walked through the remnants of an Augustinian nunnery built in 1203. I stepped over the stones, walked between the arched pink doorways, and thought of the Celtic concept of the significance of thresholds. This one was the threshold of time.

The sign at the nunnery speaks of how old the ruins are, and of what lies beneath them being older still. Of the bones that have been unearthed there.

TEAMPULL RÒNAIN
ST RONAN'S CHAPEL

This is the medieval parish church where the islanders worshipped between about 1200 and 1560. Excavations have revealed traces of an earlier chapel here, possibly dating to the 700s. Beneath were burials of an even earlier date, showing there was a thriving island population in the early days of Columba's monastery. Interestingly, all of the skeletons found in this area belonged to women.

And there you have it. More of the story is revealed with each new unearthing of the past, which reveals a deeper past, and a deeper past, and so on. Like the boxes of infinity and Paul Wallace's astrophysics, the story is larger and deeper and wider than we know or can comprehend. But there is an honor in reaching our fingers into the past as we turn our eyes to the future. That we count for something. It's more than our ancestors or the old ways. It's reconfiguring them so that they become something new. Tangible. Visible. A faith that was ancient then and may become ancient once again over the course of time, but it is up to us to make it something that stands in the gap of the present.

I walked through the doorway of pink stones. A young man sat there cross-legged in the sun, his back against the wall; another wall rose before him and served as a barrier against the wind. He wore a long braid wrapped and tied in a knot, and shorts in spite of the November cold.

"You have the best spot in the house," I told him.

He smiled and offered me a bit of conversation. He volunteered at the hostel on the other side of the isle. He was staying there now. Someone had loaned him a bike.

I wished him well and moved on, leaving him to his private contemplations.

I loved this bit about being human. The instances of intersections that were only momentary but lasted perhaps until infinity. Like the boxes. Like the characters in Kevin Brockmeier's novel *The Brief History of the Dead*, where no one ever really leaves for heaven until every last soul who has ever had the slightest interaction with them passes away from earth.

Funny how we don't realize this when we are alive. Not fully. Not until we look back in relation to the lives of others. Dead saints and poets, nuns and monks, unmarked graves, and souls resting in a potter's field.

18

Eternally Yours, Eternally Mine

We eventually left the ruins and walked up the pathway toward the abbey that had been rebuilt on the site of Columba's monastery during a revival of Iona. There is a short strip of small, quaint stores—a bicycle rental, a wool store that sells sweaters and baby goods, a small visitors center—all closed. There were no tourists out today.

The egg boy—he might have been six or seven—had indeed been at the docks upon our arrival, but he was there to greet his grandmother. He didn't bring eggs that day. He hadn't been expecting any customers. So the shops were all closed, and the eggs were packed away, and no one was biking the isle except for the lone brave soul meditating in the ruins.

At the top of the hill sits the Iona Parish Church, on the left, just off the path. I walked that way just to see, and the door was open wide, then a woman who might have been the pastor or a greeter said, "Welcome, welcome. Service is about to start. Please join us."

But I was afraid we wouldn't have time for everything else we wanted to see on the isle if we spent an hour at the worship service. I mumbled something about the ferry and the schedule and the abbey and how we really had to go, so she said, "Well, just come see, then. We haven't started yet. There's still a little time."

And that's how the three of us found ourselves in the back pew of the church, captured by the light.

The moment we entered the church and sat down—and a moment seems an odd frame of reference, a clunky way to capture an occurrence and pinpoint it on the clock, but it is this—there was the sitting. Then there was the light. And the light grew brighter. And brighter still. I had to close my eyes as I couldn't open them against the bright, and I couldn't look about the church to appreciate its beauty with eyes closed, but I wouldn't move.

I could hear two women speaking in the row in front of me, one saying, "You sit here, and I'll sit there." And then the other one saying, "We can't sit here. There's that light! We can't see anything. My goodness!" And then they were gone, searching for something more comfortable in the shadows.

From the front of the church someone began to play a Scottish tune on the violin. There are words that people use to try to describe music such as this. Words like *heavenly* and *sublime* and *supernatural*. But I had no words to describe that music. It was a key to a door that unlocked a thousand years. I began to weep.

With my eyes closed, my face held up to the light, I wept for the beautiful that was this life and the hope of glory that lay beyond it. For all those who had come before us on Iona. For Columba and his slain monks. For the nuns whose bones were buried beneath the ruins. For the holy men who came before them in a progression of pagans answering the call of Iona, paddling in carved-wood boats to set themselves apart, to serve what was sacred. For the millions who came seeking solace and searching for answers. For all the lives of all those who had come before us and for those who would come after, all in flight around the sun. Everyone just trying to get home.

When the song ended, I let each final note fade, roll, and fade again before I dared to move, open my eyes. When I did, the first thing I saw was James still sitting in the back pew there waiting for me. He joined me when I rose, and we made our way to the door and stepped outside into the sunshine together as the church bells began to ring, calling, *Come, come, one and all. The house of God is open to friend and stranger.*

"That's a very mournful piece," James said. "I saw you crying."

"Not unhappy tears," I told him.

"Joyful tears then."

"Eternal tears," I answered.

We walked up the path, searching for Virginia, and I tried to put into words what I felt. But what I felt contained too many words; they spilled out beyond the edges of description, which weakened the moment, detracted from the power of what I wanted to communicate. I tried anyway, in spite of knowing this.

"We have this great gift," I said, "which is this life. And with it comes the responsibility to live it to the fullest. Not just once but each and every day. For the sake of all the people who came before us who no longer are. We are the carriers now of this light that is called life."

Just then we found Virginia sitting on a bench between the church and the abbey.

"I had to leave," she said. "When the music began playing, I started crying, and then I was so overcome with emotion I knew I was about to break down sobbing, and I was afraid people wouldn't understand and they would worry I was ill. So, I just had to leave."

"I felt that way too," James offered, "but I tried to keep it inside and not to cry."

Later, when I returned home, a letter would arrive from James about the experience, but on that day we were just trying to keep walking. The experience had taken us all by surprise. We were just poking our heads in to get a better view of the picturesque stone church. We never expected that God would be dropping by.

I imagined—like Chloe had related about her Iona visit—that there would be people who came here during high tourist season, snapping pictures and stopping by the shops in search of souvenirs. They would look for bumper stickers that said "See Iona or Bust," like the bumper stickers and painted barns of my childhood that seemed to be everywhere and advertised, "SEE ROCK CITY." In that way, maybe people found here whatever they expected to find: Tourists found trinkets. Pilgrims found peace. We all found what we were searching for.

I looked out toward the sea and across the austere beauty that was Iona. The landscape shifted and shaped before my eyes in such a way that it seemed not only possible but probable to walk from this life straight into eternity. Like the journey of C. S. Lewis's Reepicheep, in his novel *The Voyage of the Dawn Treader*, where they reach the ends of the earth and, without natural death ever coming to him, the tiniest and bravest of them all walks directly into heaven's high forever.

19

THE LIGHT OF IONA

WE CONTINUED UP THE footpath toward the abbey and stopped by the graveyard known as Reilig Odhrain. The sign read: "Talamh Trocair, Sacred Soil." As old as the abbey itself, Iona's main burial ground is the final resting place of abbots, monks, great lords, and warriors. Story has it that it is also the resting place of forty-eight medieval Scottish kings.

There are rumors and myths about all who are buried beneath the grey headstones that rise at odd angles, slipping into the earth as it has shifted beneath them so that there is nothing uniform about them. Yet here they are, sculptures standing out against the sea and sky, scattered across the green in such an inviting way that it seems the perfect place to picnic. I can imagine us on a summer's day, a blanket laid out between the headstones, a bit of cheese and bread, a bottle of wine, keeping company with the dead in the clear blue divinity of the day.

Some say that Macbeth is buried here. Perhaps someday they might agree to house the bones of a Southern author prone to wandering in the old Celtic way, *Peregrinatio Pro Christo*.

THE CHAPEL IN THE midst of the cemetery is Caibeal Odhrain, St. Oran's Chapel, and was believed by many to be the burial chapel of the MacDonald Lords of the Isles. It was built in the 1100s and is one of the oldest intact structures on Iona. Visitors are invited to enter through the elaborately carved doorway and see the remains of an impressive tomb and a collection of exquisitely decorated West Highland grave slabs that lean against the inside wall. When I entered, I almost missed all of this. What I saw was a chapel, simple and bare, two old wooden pews, two old wooden chairs, a primitive wood cross leaning in the corner, unmounted and unadorned.

In the left corner, prayer candles burned, and I lit another in the name of James's mother and her memory. There was a little white stone altar with a small gold metal Celtic cross fixed behind it; a red candle sat at the center, burning, the sign of eternity. There was a small, intricately carved hearth where one could build a fire, and one tiny window, high up and recessed, that afforded the light a chance to enter. The floor was bare, cut stone, precisely the way it might have been hundreds of years ago. It all seemed untouched, as if the family had, only moments ago, taken communion and gone for a stroll, the lit candles still burning as evidence of their recent prayers.

At each place we entered I wished to linger, but the abbey was waiting, and soon the ferry would return to collect us.

We entered the grounds of the abbey and were greeted by the sight of the tall, sculpted, and engraved "high cross," this Celtic symbol that had come to mean more to me with each passing day. More than just the thing I wear about my neck, more than just the endpiece of my prayer beads. I was standing in the place of its beginning. This message of Christ's coming and crucifixion, revelation and resurrection, and the circle of the sun and eternal life.

The abbey itself was so impressively built of stone that it seemed as if it could suffer all the winds and winter storms of the Outer Hebrides and still stand, no worse for wear.

We found the heavy, arched wooden doors unlocked, like all the doors of Mull. I pulled off my backpack and gladly left it resting in a chair at the back, shoved my hands deep in the pockets of my jacket as I walked through the silent abbey. There were stone arches and alcoves and corners, and in this house of holy, I took out my phone and snapped a few shots of the cross at the window, the stone arches and ceiling, and the statue of Columba. I hesitate to take photos in churches of any kind, but this time I made an exception. I wanted to hold onto the memories and be able to use them for reference. Now, months later, when I view them, every photo—every cross, archway, or token left by a fellow pilgrim—seems a work of art.

Virginia had gone off to explore the island in what little time we had left, but James sat silent in the rear of the church, his wool cap on and his head hung down, as if he was deep asleep, like an ancient angel, a guardian of the gate.

There are services in the abbey every day of the week except Sunday. There are morning services and healing services and communion services. But we were there on Sunday. No services of any kind. So I found myself alone in the Abbey of Iona, walking in the light that spilled through the arched windows, listening to the still, small voice within me that offered nothing more profound than—*I am home.* And here in this place I felt a peace that passed all understanding. I was not shadowed by worry or hurry. I was not concerned about how far I had come for such a short amount of time or that I didn't have days to be on the island or to sit in the abbey.

Now was all the time I needed.

I walked slowly from the nave to the chancel and back again, into the alcove that housed the sculpture dedicated to Columba, and what had once been the feet of his statue. It is said that touching them will offer miracles. I touched them, held my fingers there, wished for miracles for everyone.

The stairs that led up to the monks' quarters had a rope across them, with a sign that said "Please do not enter." There was also a plaque that read:

STAIDHRE OIDHCHE
Night Stair

This was a short cut between the abbey church and the dormitory. The monks filed sleepily down these steps every night for matins services held at 3 a.m.

I walked back and forth, exploring, and passed James the sentry, unmoving, eyes closed, head down. I discovered the places where pilgrims had left stones and shells, tiny feathers, and other offerings behind. I had nothing to offer but my words, and I added my single, silent prayer request.

Let the light of Iona live in my heart.
Let the light of Iona live in my heart.
Let the light of Iona live in my heart.

When I returned to the back of the nave, James opened his eyes and stood, ready to go. I strapped on my pack, and we went out in search of Virginia.

We stopped at Cumhdach Chaluim Cille, St. Columba's Shrine. The graves of saints are always at risk of being ransacked for parts and portions of their remains, any element that can be ransomed to produce a miracle. And those in need of a miracle don't always question the methods or means by which it arrives. Columba's protection was the tiniest of stone chapels reconstructed in the likeness of what was, in the 800s, an elaborately decorated, wooden shrine built around the grave. There have been reports of sightings of heavenly lights and angels, but these weren't on display when we paid our respects.

We found Virginia taking pictures, and we all picked up the path that led down toward the dock. Eventually, we arrived, tired and cold, and searched for a place that would shelter us a bit from the wind. We chose the storefront of the closed bicycle shop, and James divided up our small sandwiches, which we ate quickly. Then one of us discovered one last piece of bread, another a small bottle of wine that no one remembered purchasing. Virginia broke the bread into three pieces and passed it to us, then she opened the wine, and since we had no cups, we passed the bottle around.

"It's like we're taking communion," James said in his lilting voice.

"Yes," I said, "from a common cup."

I could think of no better way to leave Iona than with this blessing.

PART
4

TIME IS A TRAVELER

. . . the never-ending flight of future days . . .
—JOHN MILTON

The past is but the beginning of a beginning, and all that is and has been is but the twilight of the dawn.
—H. G. WELLS

In a real dark night of the soul it is always three o'clock in the morning.
—F. SCOTT FITZGERALD

20

SUDDENLY STRANGERS

T HEN SUDDENLY THE FERRY arrived, and we were whisked away. Churning back across the cold water, back to Mull and the one-way road that James would navigate to get us back to Oban, to another ferry, and across the only road to Glasgow. Back through the snow-capped mountains and past the sheep in the fields.

We had planned to journey on to Aberdeen to stay with PhD students who had offered to open their home to us, but when taking a closer look at our route so that we could accept Malcolm Guite's invitation to visit Cambridge, we realized those first plans just wouldn't work out. I was touched by the sincere disappointment of the students who had offered their hospitality and whom we would not meet in person. I felt disappointed too. As if I were missing a great visit with an old friend, not just missing a convenient place to drop my pack and sleep.

Originally, we were to spend two nights with James and then part ways after our trip to Iona, but that had changed on the way. Now we were heading all the way back to Glasgow, where we would spend another night together before Virginia and I picked up our route back toward England and returned home. James had been a part of the divine plan all along. He was on pilgrimage too.

We traveled down the one-way across the Isle of Mull, past the long-haired *Heilan coo* and the sheep. I longed to reach my arm out the window as if I could sweep it across the landscape, to memorize it and hold it to me.

Finally, we were almost to the docks. Night had fallen, and we were hungry, thirsty, and tired. James stopped at the first place we found near the docks, a small pub attached to an inn. We wanted to hurry and eat and grab a drink, before the ferry and then the long drive back through the empty landscape to Glasgow, with little more than the beauty of the wilderness of Scotland and its ice-capped peaks.

Then we made the only social faux pas of the entire journey, for which we would love to apologize to our fellow Americans. It was the only time we didn't represent with grace and good manners.

When we entered the pub, it appeared to have only one bartender to take orders, no wait staff. It was a small place, and the bar was encircled with men who stood shoulder to shoulder. Virginia and I both grew up in a tourist town on the Florida coast. We were raised with good manners, knew how to say please and thank you and wait our turn. There must have been some sort of memory code of younger days when the smell of suntan oil was our only perfume, and where, in the hundred-percent humidity and covered in sand, you learned to navigate an outside bar full of spring-breakers from around the nation. Like all locals, we knew how to break through the tourists lined up four rows deep and not wait an hour for a Coke. Unfortunately, some sort of flashbacks must have ensued, and we shoved ourselves through the men like halfbacks on a football team.

These men were locals who had stopped for a pint on the way home. Fishermen or clam divers, maybe construction workers. They were that kind of "men's men." I knew them. They were the men of my family. The orchard workers and cotton pickers and sawmill workers. The rough-and-tumble men of my childhood. But these men saw me as a pushy American. They didn't know that I was like them. That I came from the same neighborhood. I knew their dreams. A roof, a full belly, a well child, a warm family. And the things they didn't have time for. The frivolous talk of people who don't work with their hands for a living.

James had gone quietly to sit by the fire in the corner. He knew the men at the bar too. They were also the men of his childhood, but now he was worlds away from his past. A psychiatrist with a flat in Glasgow.

We grabbed pints and carried them to the table after the men reformed a wall strong enough to keep us from the bar. It was the only place from city streets to backwater isles where we hadn't been welcomed with open arms and big smiles and stories.

I sat sipping the beer, waiting on food, and thought, We'll do better next time. We'll be quiet and slow and respect that circle that you've formed, your wall against the world. We'll sit by the fire and wait for a turn, for someone to speak. We won't intrude on this holy space you have carved out for yourselves.

I made a mental note. I would have another someday.

Columba knew what he was doing when he came up the Irish coast to evangelize the Scottish with his Christ. This is how he did it: carefully. He didn't knock on doors and pass out pamphlets. No, he came with twelve disciples. And the disciples went out among the people but not proselytizing. They went out and built lean-tos and huts among the tribal areas, and they lived among the people. Drank and ate and laughed with them. Worked alongside them. And the people came to know them and to trust them. Then little by little they spoke of this God, this Christ, this Christian way.

Columba would have known to walk slowly into that pub, to nod with respect to the barkeep and the men who stood, burly and tired and worn, having a word and a pint away from their work and their women. He would have moved slowly to sit in the corner by the fire until someone decided it was time to take his order. And something of his kindness, his light, his peace might have led one of them to ask for his story. To ask where he was from and why he happened to be so far from home and in their midst. And upon hearing him speak, they would know he was a friend to be welcomed.

One day, someday, I'd return and in the spirit of Columba, I'd make my way to the fire.

21

THE DANCE
OF ST. JAMES

HOURS LATER, TIRED AND spent, we arrived in Glasgow. The city had a good feel. As if the moment you entered it, the city was glad you had returned safely. I thought of the Celtic tribes moving this way and that, being in touch with the earth, and I wondered if this is how they decided when and where to stop. The few recorded notes about their habits said their wanderings and ramblings appeared to be random, but maybe it was like the welcome of Glasgow. Maybe the land spoke to them, welcomed them as if it knew their names. If this were true, then they were sensitive in the way the monks were to the voice of God. And in Celtic

147

Christianity, being sensitive to the voice of God manifesting in all creation was the natural way. I wanted to know how I could tap into that same wisdom. Make my decisions by such instinct. I didn't always know where the journey would take me or why. I didn't always know the way I would take to get there or the people who would somehow, beyond all reason, come together to bring me to the holy ground of my life where I was meant to stand. I could not and would not know these things in advance of the fullness of their revelation. I could only hope to arrive at the simple truth that God held the threads of my life in hand, and if I would follow the gentle whisper, the songline, the gentle sound of those bells, moment by moment I would find myself stepping into the fullness of the destiny of my days.

We pulled up in front of James's flat, where we unloaded our bags, and James, thankfully, offered to carry my pack up the flights of stairs. After we had showered and changed, he cooked pasta and bread and opened a bottle of red wine. It would be our last meal together, and we were all aware of this and were experiencing a touch of sadness. We were not the same people upon returning that we'd been a few days before. The quest had bound us together, revealed our strengths, our intellect, our humor, and our spirituality. It had reminded us that we were indeed parts of a whole. Four days ago, we had been strangers. Now that felt like a lifetime ago.

St. James, as we had begun fondly calling him, poured the wine and said, "Isn't it something? The people we pass that are only in our lives for a moment, but in spite of that, they're there forever. They become a part of us. Like Brian, the ferry bartender, and Gillian, the innkeeper, and the ferry boat captain."

"And the egg boy of Iona," I said. "And his grandmother, who booked the ferry."

"And that wonderful, white-haired old man that worked in the store at the pass," Virginia added. He had told us great stories and been so happy for us to visit his store that he delayed us an extra thirty minutes. He would have kept us all evening. Carried us home.

"The waitress in Oban," I said. She was a young college student, with a round, soft smile, and so eager to please, to do a good job. She'd taken a photo of the three of us, fish and chips before us, a candle on the table, and you'd never realize, looking at that shot, that we were navigating the cold and the missed ferries, the dark roads, delays, and the flat tire. You wouldn't see it. Just three friends out for a warm, wonderful dinner. Pictures can be deceiving, but they can also reveal the truth that lies below the surface.

"And Leon," added Virginia, "don't forget Leon."

We all raised our glasses in a toast to Leon, who "never fucking wouldn't stop" to help someone. Who dove for clams in the cold, dark sea so that he could feed his family— a wife and four children. And we prayed for God to bless him and keep him all of his days.

Then we let our imaginations wander, played match-maker for Gillian, who had mentioned that she had little chance of meeting a man on the Isle of Mull as she tended the sheep. James wondered how it might be if maybe Brian should somehow meet her. "I think," said James, "he'd get her to stop working so hard all the time. That he would say, 'Let it be tonight, Gillian. Just let it all be. We'll just light a fire in the hearth and sit by the warm.'"

We painted word pictures for James for when he came to America. How we would take him first to this place and then to that. Virginia told him about the tall green trees along the Oregon coast and how he would love biking through the city of Portland. I told him of the American West and Route 66. Of my love of the Four Corners and high deserts and Taos and Santa Fe.

"A good trip across the country," I said. "That's really what you need."

We both told him about where we were from in the Deep South, that we would throw a party for him so he could meet all our friends, and about how all the women would love the way he said, "Thanking you kindly, ma'am," in his Scottish accent.

Then James asked us what music we would like to hear. He put on some old Southern rock, then played Delbert McClinton's "Rosy" for Virginia. James and I remained at the table talking about places to roam, but she began dancing around the room, not the least bit self-conscious. I loved this about my friend. The way she could dance with joy anywhere, anytime. Surely the Celtic people were like this too. And so was the spiritual thread of Christianity that came from Columba, with all of its divine joy in God's creation. In believing we were born with the goodness of God within us, carrying that vision of St. John the Beloved listening to the heartbeat of God.

The three of us celebrated the end of the pilgrimage for James and the continuing pilgrimage for us. Celebrated the taking of chances, the making of new friends, the traveling of unknown roads, searching for God, and meeting God on Iona.

Then James introduced us to Michael Kiwanuka, put on his song "One More Night," and Virginia, still dancing, took James's hand and pulled him up from the table. He rose, and they began to dance together. One leading and the other following, shifting, changing places, the other leading, the other following. Virginia and St. James were alive and dancing, and I was watching them in the room and in their reflections in the window, blending with the expansive view of the city. The lights blinked like hot, white stars behind them as they circled the room again and again, and my heart ignited, caught fire, and burned so deeply I felt I could fly. I wanted to take a picture; I wanted to say something, but I remained transfixed, did not move or join their invitation to the dance. I was dancing in my soul, not wanting to move so that time might stop and there would always be this moment—Virginia and James eternally laughing, twirling, and I was so overcome with thankfulness for the road that called to the deep waters of possibility, for the road that brought us back again, and the miracle of all of it unfolding before me that I stayed rooted in my place, watching them twirl and laugh and sway to the beat.

I read in Robert Macfarlane's *The Old Ways* about a friend telling Robert that he abhorred Christianity of any kind except for the early Celtic Christian church, in which, he declared, "ale was libated to the sea to increase the fertility of the seaweed and the fish, there was new-moon worship, [and] there was dancing."

I wasn't there. I don't know for a fact that the early Celtic church did any of that. But I do know I can celebrate the rising of the new moon. That if the fish want to drink beer, I say let them, and let there be blessings and benedictions said over all our dusty corners and dancing 'til the dawn. Let our incantation be the act of living a passionate life filled with celebration that we offer like a living sacrifice unto the God of all creation.

THE NEXT MORNING, I would rise early, stand at the window looking out over Glasgow with my coffee and beads in hand, praying as the others still slept. Later, when they awoke, we would tell James goodbye as he left early for his office. We would wash dishes, make beds, sweep floors, vacuum rooms, wipe down counters. We would pack our bags, double-check our room, and take one last look at the view, say a prayer, a benediction, for the good life of St. James.

We'd leave his key in the dish on the table and close the door to flat number 7. We would descend the stairs and step out into the cold morning light of Glasgow.

That evening James would return home to his flat and find it clean, cold, and dark. There would be no remaining traces of us, no sign that we had existed except for the ghost of our presence, like an energy that ran through the Abbey of Iona. That would linger and stay, rise at odd times and whisper, *Remember.*

22

THE STONE OF DESTINY

WE LEFT THE STREET of St. James and walked down toward the University of Glasgow, past the fountains and statues in the park. People bundled in coats and babies snuggled in prams filled the sidewalks, even their dogs donning sweaters against the cold, and we could hear people speaking in the soft, rolling poetry of the Gaelic tongue. I did not understand much of what they said in passing, but I loved the lilting, musical notes of their words. The sun was shining, and this seemed to make the intensity of the cold a trick of the mind.

At James's flat, the wide windows had afforded a space for all the warmth of the sun's rays, and as we had gone into our scrubbing of pans and fluffing of pillows, we'd worked up a sweat. Like Gillian, the shepherd of the sheep, we'd warmed up with little need of a fire, but now that we were back on the streets, the wind was biting. The long journey to Iona and back, the late evening of celebration, and the duties of being diligent to leave James's place as tidy as we'd found it had us ready for a rest. It would be hours before Gail was home in Edinburgh to let us in to her home. The train ride was only an hour or so, so we decided to spend a few last hours in the city that had come to feel like home.

I looked at the stone buildings surrounding the campus, at for-rent signs placed in the windows of apartments, and wondered how much it would cost for a writer to find something just for a month to hole up and write. I looked at help-wanted signs for baristas and bartenders and thought, *I could do that. Tend bar at night. Write during the day. Live in Glasgow, Scotland, where I could catch a train to the isles and a ferry back to the Isle of Iona and hang out with the ghosts of the saints and martyrs.* Or perhaps the Glasgow University would have a dorm room open for such as me. A writer needing a sabbatical. I could teach on the side. I could offer a course on American slang and the cultural relevance of the '70s and '80s featured in programs like *That '70s Show* and *Stranger Things*. I was willing to be creative and invent all sorts of hybrid writing classes for a ticket to return.

We also had other business to attend to. We were broke. Like some American sitcom we referred to as *Two Broke Girls in Glasgow*. The exchange rate at the airport had practically divided our travel funds by two. We had half the cash we had planned on, and although we found everything in Scotland more than reasonable and affordable, we still didn't have the funds we had intended. A friend was wiring us additional money by Western Union. Thank God for good friends and fast cash.

We located a Western Union office and proudly walked to the store, only to find the gate closed and a sign that read something about the store being relocated. We walked up and down the street looking for signs of the new location, to no avail, and popped into a tiny shop that sold a little bit of everything you might need. Scotch was behind the cash register, as was ibuprofen. It was the equivalent of the 7-Eleven of my childhood, minus the scotch.

The young man behind the counter had an infectious smile, and his welcome seemed as genuine as could be. So did the change of his face when we asked about the money.

"I'm sorry but they've closed," he said.

We told him we knew, but we needed to find the new store. That's when he went on to explain they had all closed. Most likely in all of Scotland. Some kind of problem or disagreement, and now he thought they were *all* closed. (Another note to self: Do not go broke in Scotland and need a wire from Western Union.)

These were lessons you usually learned in process. There was no way to prepare for everything in advance. Like life, you had to roll with it and do the best you could to get down the next block. We had our train tickets already purchased for Edinburgh and for Cambridge. We had a few pounds left. The point now was not to panic. And to find a pub.

We had passed a place earlier when we were in search of the Western Union, and we worked our way back down the street in that direction until we found the pub on the corner. The sign above the door read "The Arlington." We walked inside, and it was precisely what a good Scottish pub should be. It had a few tables and a bar that was long and mostly empty, save a guy reading the paper at the end with a pint, and a man at the bar in full traditional Scottish dress. White hair and white beard, cap with a feather, kilt, sporran, kilt hose, and ghillies. *Well, now,* I thought, *going old school.*

The man behind the bar, about my age, with dark hair up in a bun and glasses, gave us a smile. Not wanting to make the same mistake we'd made in the pub by the docks, I asked, "What is proper for us to do here? Would you like us to order at the bar? To sit at a table? We want to be sure we get it right, whatever it is."

"You can sit where you like, and you're welcome to stand at the bar. If you do, hop on one leg," he said with a smile.

I showed him I was good for it and could indeed, in spite of the weight of my pack, hop on one leg. He laughed and asked, "What'll it be?"

I told him two pints, and as he pulled them, he asked if we were on holiday.

"Not really," I said. "Just returned from Iona."

His expression changed, took on a look of respect.

"Ahh, pilgrimage then."

"Yes, a pilgrimage."

"It's my daughter's name. Iona. I named her for the isle."

Of all the gin joints in all the world, I thought, we walked into this one.

Then in a greater rush of enthusiasm he said some other things that I tried hard to understand, never did, and didn't ask him to repeat. I took the pints to the table and looked up to discover the album cover of *Abbey Road* with the Beatles crossing the street to enter the Arlington. Turns out the iconic photo was taken in London, so apparently someone had worked a little photo-editing magic.

Then I turned to see Virginia with her hand on a huge stone that sat in a niche in the wall, a light on it changing hues of crystal green. The sign above it read: "The Stone of Destiny." Then it told the story.

The Stone of Destiny was a carved seat used for the coronation of Scottish kings and queens until it was stolen by the English king Edward I and taken to Westminster Abbey in 1296. On Christmas Day in 1950, four patriotic Glasgow University students stole the Stone of Destiny from Westminster Abbey. When they returned to Glasgow, they went to the Arlington Bar for a celebratory pint and hoisted the stone onto the bar top. Most people believe the stone was returned to Westminster in 1951 and is now on display in Edinburgh Castle, but the pub owners believe otherwise. The students made a replica of the stone, which they passed off as the original, and hid the real Stone of Destiny in the

Arlington Bar beneath a boxed pub seat. It is now proudly on display for all to see.

I touched the Stone of Destiny, thought of Iona and the bar owner's daughter, and then sat at the table beneath the poster of the Beatles supposedly walking into this very pub so many years ago. The man in the Scottish kilt hadn't been very friendly when we entered, but when he learned we had been on pilgrimage, he changed his tune and was ready to share a multitude of stories about his traditional dress and why he wore it. About his family and his clan and his feather. Virginia began to speak with him about both her Scottish and her Native American heritage. Then he saw my Celtic cross and told me how much he liked it and began a story about the ancient Celts, and I was trying to understand, and then it occurred to me that if he liked the cross, I could show him something else.

"I've got something to show you," I said, "something I think you'll like." As I pulled off my coat, then my scarf, and my sweater, he sat in rapt attention. Then I slid the collar of my shirt down off my shoulder and showed him my tattoo.

"Ahh, that's nice," he said. "You've got the sign of the Celtic tribe."

The bar owner spoke up from behind the bar where he'd been reading the newspaper. He slid his glasses down on his nose, looked over them, and told us more than I will ever know because I got only every fourth word.

Then he said something about how he had his DNA tested, and he was excited to find that he was part Native American because, apparently, back in the days of the shipping industry, the Scottish men would work on the ships, and they would go to America, and sometimes they found Native American wives and would bring them back to Scotland. So, many people discovered they had Native American blood, and they were very proud of that.

That much I got. But when talk of the Rosslyn Chapel surfaced and the Knights Templar and how they were still around today and what they did in secret and so forth—I couldn't understand a word he said. "Knights Templar . . . today . . . secrets . . . all true." These were the things that were clear to me. The rest of it was music. A beautiful tune that I loved but could never decipher. *This*, I thought, *is going to take some time. I will simply have to come here and stay. To live with this day after day. This is the only way that I will ever truly understand.*

Just like other things in life: I didn't understand communion by watching other people take communion. I didn't get the benefits of yoga by practicing downward-facing dog for three minutes once a month. And I wouldn't understand Celtic Christianity by sitting quietly for a few minutes one day a week, by walking the rounds the next, or wearing a Celtic cross on Fridays. To embrace the discipline of yoga and receive the maximum benefits, I had to practice it daily and understand the history, logic, spirituality, focus of it. Same with Celtic Christianity.

The trick to it is no trick at all. It's a commitment. I was learning that if you loved God in the way that the Celtic Christians did, then you were all in. You didn't live your life practicing a few bullet points based on the spiritual highlights of the Celtic Christians. You became them, and they became you. They were so integrated into your life that there was no separating your life from theirs. It was who you were.

23

TIME WILL TELL

LET US SPEAK NOW of time, of its mystery and magnificence. There have been three instances in my life when time took on another dimension, a quality that felt tangibly different than ordinary time.

The first was many years ago, when my sons were but babies. My sister and I had been in a small boat fishing with my father on the edge of a creek, just by the landing. My grandparents' old house sat but a few yards up from the water, and there on the porch my mother was rocking the baby, singing softly to him. My sister, my father, and I, the three of us, sat in the boat without speaking, cane fishing poles in hand, red corks dancing in the wind on the surface of the water. Occasionally one of us would raise our line out of the water, check that a worm still dangled from the hook, then slowly lower it back beneath the surface. The cicadas were singing with the wind the particular song that is theirs and theirs alone. When the breeze picked up a little, they would become silent until it stopped, then their song would rise again, remain. During this time, I knew as I was sitting there that there was something eternal about that moment. As if we had somehow stepped into a pocket of time where time itself did not exist or where it had paused. The Celtic people would have called this threshold that felt otherworldly, or of a different dimension somehow, a thin place.

Some people say the standing stones of Callanish in northern Scotland mark a thin place, and others say Stonehenge is one. In the States, Sedona, Arizona, is sometimes said to be a thin place, but the fact of the matter is that one who is sensitive to such things would know it regardless of location. And maybe on that day with my father and sister in the boat, my mother rocking on the porch with my sons, we had created the opening to a thin place ourselves. Regardless of how it happened, I know it did.

Another time was what I mentioned earlier, when I had the opportunity to stay with some friends at a solitary house on a deserted island. Arrival on the island felt as eternal as the stay there. Even the ceremony of taking off our watches and placing them in a closet for the duration marked those days as leaving the daily demands behind and entering into island time, what I understood as the time of God.

This time it had been the trip to Iona. That night when we were sitting around James's table eating dinner, I said, "It feels as if we've been gone weeks, not days. Like we have gone through some type of time warp." Everyone agreed. It was as if what we had experienced could not have been done in that length of time. And yet—it had.

I was something of a self-taught student regarding time, in that I read voraciously such works as Carlo Rovelli's *The Order of Time*, Alan Lightman's *Searching for Stars on an Island in Maine*, and Nicholas Mee's *The Cosmic Mystery Tour*. Every woman has to have a hobby, and studying time and theoretical physics is mine. This was one of the things that drew me to the Celtic nature. The Celtic people understood time differently.

My own personal experiences were what had created this longing to read and understand—coupled with another thing Celtic people trusted in: dreams. They give dreamtime its due and believe that God can communicate with someone through dreams and that heeding those messages is highly worthwhile.

Several years ago, I had a dream about time I have never forgotten. It was a dream unlike any I'd ever had or have had since in that it was completely realistic. It felt as if I were actually at that place in that time on that day. And what was pressing me most in the dream was the sense that I had been away from home for too long and my children wouldn't know where I was. That I needed to get back to them. But I was inspired to look down at my watch in this dream, and when I did, it was a glorious gold watch with four hands instead of two. I understood with a certain quickness that there were two types of time—humanity's time and God's time—and that I was currently in God's time and therefore had nothing to worry about.

The trip to Iona had felt that way, as if we had moved in God's time and had been gone for weeks, but now, returning to Glasgow, we were back in human time again.

So, it was in human time that we returned to Gail's home for a night with her on our way to Cambridge, breaking her "two nights only" rule, and she opened the door to us with, "Welcome home!" Back up to our room on the fourth floor, and I tried not to grumble about the stairs. It seemed in Scotland every place you needed to be was either up or down from where you were standing.

The next morning, after a breakfast of eggs and smoked salmon, Gail was determined to help us find a Western Union and collect our money, so she drove us to one location after another only to discover that what we had been told appeared true. It seemed that the Western Union was closed in all of Scotland.

And that's when we missed the train.

We took what remained of our dwindling funds and repurchased the tickets to Cambridge with a connection in St. Petersburg. We'd arrive just thirty minutes prior to the Fellows dinner Malcolm Guite had invited us to. All the while, I kept repeating, "All shall be well, and all shall be well, and all manner of thing shall be well," trying not to panic now after we'd come so far.

We went to the only place open to sit in the train station: the pub. A sign on the wall said, "The train can wait! There's always time for another beer." We ordered a pint and waited.

24

COLUMBA AT CAMBRIDGE

Once en route on the train, we watched the countryside roll, change, and fade with the light; night fell as the accents of the people around us shifted from the Scottish lilt to the sing-song properness of British English.

When Malcolm had written a note saying that he and his wife, Maggie, could host us for an evening, I was delighted. It meant that I could visit, however briefly, with an old colleague from The Kindlings, an international organization founded by Dick Staub and Nigel Goodwin. I'd had the pleasure of presenting at the Kindlingsfest on Orcas

Island, Washington, a few years ago and heard Malcolm tell a wonderful story about Iona.

He had shared with attendees a marvelous tale about how, many years ago, when he was a young man searching for what he believed or disbelieved about God, he simply took off and hiked up the Scottish coast, emerging weeks later out of the woods and into a clearing where bonfires burned. The Scots there welcomed him, offered him a drink made from potatoes, something akin to our Southern moonshine back home. Malcolm sat with them and explained that he had come on this journey searching for evidence of the Divine, and they told him, "Well, of course you've come to us today. God has brought you here. It's the feast day of your namesake, Columba." (The name *Malcolm* comes from Scots Gaelic, *Máel Coluim,* meaning "disciple of St. Columba.")

Malcolm spent time with them, and in their joyous celebration of Christianity and their welcoming hospitality he saw something he felt he could relate to. Even possibly embrace. So he went down to the beach alone and spoke this:

"Christ, I am not a Christian, nor do I intend to ever become a Christian, but should I ever do so, I will travel to the mission of Columba, to Iona, and make my vow to you there."

Three years later, on the Isle of Iona, on his knees, Malcolm took his vows.

So it was that Virginia and I found ourselves having dinner at Cambridge with someone who had been named after Columba and who had taken his vows on Iona. What a wild and wonderful thing! And, since Malcolm and Maggie were hosting the Fellows dinner that evening, we found ourselves at the head table, where we were informed dinner would be followed by a compline (night prayer) service in the chapel, which would feature Gregorian chant; if that were of interest to us, we were most welcome to join.

I was fond of Gregorian chant and found it soothing. Once, during the middle of a project and facing a tight deadline, I'd gone into a used-record store and declared, "I need some Gregorian monks STAT!" (The record store guy had said they kept chanting monks in the back room.)

Malcolm's vows, Gregorian chant, dinner at the head table in Cambridge—it was all some strange Iona icing on the cake. Like God was throwing me a pilgrimage party.

After dinner we adjourned for dessert and port by the fire, where my attention was caught by a large painting of a beautiful woman, her dress hanging just off her shoulders, dark hair flowing, eyes flashing, and all of her poised as if her spirit were exclaiming that she was wild and free. She looked like a saint of the dance, and that was a saint I would follow.

Compline signals the completion of the day. It follows the tradition of canonical hours, and in many monasteries, it is followed by a period known as the great silence, when no words are spoken until morning. It tends to be a contemplative service that emphasizes spiritual peace. I could imagine the monks of Iona at their evening prayers and the peaceful silence to follow. It would have been the silence of an abbey built of wood and with a thatched roof, standing near the water. Which would have meant a silence filled with the sounds of the wind and the calling of night birds and, in the distance, water lapping the shore, bubbling over the rocks and the shells before it receded into the sea.

The service was held by candlelight, each of us holding a lit candle to add our light to the darkness while the Gregorian chant rose and lowered in angelic waves. Holy, holy, holy. Peace on earth, indeed.

Afterward, Malcolm and Maggie drove us to their home, where with great pride, he told me of his grandmother, who wrote stories and had a book published. It was in verse, and it featured none other than Columba of Iona, after whom Malcolm's grandmother had named him. And I sat at their kitchen table trying to comprehend this turn of events. My being here in Cambridge at this kitchen table, only to find Columba here waiting.

Malcolm went to his library and pulled the treasured volume from a shelf, laid it before me at the kitchen table. Malcolm and Maggie and Virginia all said their goodnights and went off to bed. But not me. It was like Christmas morning and I'd unwrapped Iona. I remained there in the kitchen, with Malcolm's grandmother by way of her book, *A Legendary of St. Mungo* by Janetta I. W. Murray. Dedicated to her husband, "J.H.M., Who Disbelieves in Legends and Disapproves of Saints."

I turned the first page and began.

It started with a list of the principal characters. The final character and the title of the last chapter was "Columba. Abbot of Iona, Missionary and Saint."

I opened the book at random and began reading from page 121, "The Choral Song of the Monks."

Dreams compel their own fruition;
Freed from time and space he knows
Past and future of each soul,
How to counsel and control.

Right then, right there, I stopped worrying about song-lines slipping away from me or that I might mess up and miss out on the synergy of bread crumbs, the little signs and wonders along the way. I simply followed.

The next morning Malcolm picked up Gail's mission of locating an open Western Union. Thankfully, they were open in England and had a Cambridge office. As he was driving us there, I asked him to please share with Virginia the story of his soul-searching summer, when he'd simply taken off, left Ireland, and walked north along the coastline all the way.

25

THere Are MessenGers

IF COLUMBA HAD BEEN waiting for me in Cambridge, I couldn't imagine who would show up at our last stop before we flew out of London the following day. I did know that I was more than delighted that I'd be spending the day with my former editor from Jericho Books, who'd moved to England. I had that strange sense of going by an old friend's house on the way home. A girl from the Deep South going to see a girl from the Deep South half a world away. Wearing the same jeans for two weeks and my old boots, I felt just like a princess at the ball. I'd been wined and dined, had ridden a coach to Iona; I'd stood in one of the thinnest, most divine places on planet earth, heard angels sing, and discovered new treasures. What more could there be? I didn't know, but I knew that I needed nothing else. The trip had been magical, the pilgrimage life-changing.

The train pulled into Uckfield Station, and there was beautiful Wendy Grisham, wearing a big smile as she waved to us. Then she drove us to her little cottage in the picturesque village of East Sussex.

Wendy is a Mississippi native, her accent all sugar-sweet drawl, and completely English at the same time. After dinner at her favorite pub, we settled in her living room in front of her roaring fireplace and told stories of our travels. I recounted the day of the eclipse and what it was like for totality to engulf Nashville. We pulled out our phones and all searched the locations and date for the next great eclipse. We decided we would all meet in Northern Spain in August 2026. It wasn't that far away, and it wasn't too early to come up with a plan. It was worth every mile, and I thought that would give me a chance to return to Iona and go to Holy Island while I was at it.

Wendy and I stayed up late into the evening talking about writing and the business of publishing, life and friendships, London and the future. I had asked to sleep on the sofa that defied description of how large and soft and snuggly it was. She tucked me in, something no one's done for many years, blanket upon blanket, and I felt the warm glow of the fire as it popped and crackled—the exact kind of thing that would lull any tired traveler into a deep sleep. But not this one, not that night.

I lay awake thinking of the entire trip and how we would finally be flying home tomorrow. I recounted each step along the way, the kindnesses and considerations that had been shown us. The bonding and making of friendships that would last forever. And how, at the end of my travels, here I was in Wendy's home, with its warmth and its charm and the sweetness of her familiarity.

In spite of the fact that we had to be up by six to leave for London, I dozed for only a little while and couldn't get back to sleep.

An hour later I wrote these words in my journal:

It's four as the crow flies over the ocean blue. All is quiet on this hill in this village in this cottage. The women upstairs are sleeping, and I've been awake since three—the hour monks once rose from their sleep to wander down the stone stairs of the Abbey of Iona to sing prayers and praise to God. My mind is filled with anticipating going home and work to be done, but I don't want to lose a moment of the divine magic of this journey. I have added logs to the fire and poured the tiniest sip in a precious glass of Wendy's of this elixir they seem quite fond of here that they all call single malt, and there is something about this one being "gently aged for sixteen years" in a special cask. But what does this small-town girl know about such things? Only that the fire burns as my friends sleep sweetly up the stairs. I searched Wendy's bookshelf to find something I might read that would be the perfect companion for these dark hours waiting for the dawn. And much to my surprise as I moved from one title to another, there was one I recognized.

The Messenger of Magnolia Street. In it the author has written an inscription to her friend, Wendy Grisham, about the magic of God finding us in all the right places. And so it is that I've come to this journey's end where my own words have circled back around to find me. An ocean away from where I wrote them years ago, an ocean away from where I gave this friend this book in a Nashville restaurant one evening over dinner, and yet here it is, in all its first-edition hardback glory as beautiful to me as the day she was born and came into the earth. So I settle by the fire and lift this glass to God's great magic and all the wonder of the holy mystery we call life. I turn the page and settle back as the recording angel of all that ever was or shall be begins his story:

> *God was walking through Shibboleth. His hands were in his pockets, and he was rummaging through time, the distant past and the near future.*

PART 5

IONA ON THE HILL

First keep the peace within yourself, then you can also bring peace to others.

—THOMAS À KEMPIS

Peace is not an absence of war; it is a virtue, a state of mind, a disposition for benevolence, confidence, justice.

—BENEDICT SPINOZA

Sloppy, raggedy-assed old life. I love it. I never want to die.

—DENNIS TRUDELL

26

Every Step a Prayer

Wendy had taken care to ensure we would make our way back to London, catching multiple trains and the tube to Paddington Station, where we would catch the final train to Heathrow Airport. Along the way we were informed that our flight would be delayed, so we tarried in the souvenir shop and stopped at a restaurant to eat—until I looked up to get an update on our flight information and was shocked to read: "The doors are now closing."

Naturally, what ensued was a Lucy-and-Ethel moment as we ran screaming through the airport and caught the tram to the gate that led to the escalators. Of course our departing gate was the very last one. We heard a man yell,

"Nashville?!!!" And out of breath, we managed to scream a resounding "Yes, yes! That's us!"

To which he replied, "Don't worry. All is well. The main thing is you have arrived, and see, the plane is still here, and we were just getting everyone comfortable, so you're actually right on time." At least that's what I would have *liked* for him to have said, but apparently he wasn't having a very good day and we were the straw that broke the poor, metaphorical camel's back, and he chided us for being late in spite of our saying, "But you were the ones who said *you* were late."

To which he informed us that now we had caused "one hundred and fifty-two people to sit on the plane waiting."

And this was how we were welcomed back to reality. Our trip home began as I thought, *Only one hundred and fifty-two? This is a mighty small plane to fly back across the ocean blue.*

But the frustration of the ticket man was not shared by the lovely British Airlines attendants, who met us at the plane door with smiles and a genuine welcome, calming us with their words and helping us find our seats. For the return trip I had not been able to book our seats together, and a young couple watched me approaching with my heavy pack on my back. I gave them a sheepish smile that said, "Yes, you lucked out and got me. Here we go."

At my row, I said, "See this pack? I've worn it for two weeks, and I can't get it up in those bins without help." And a young man about the age of my son stepped up from a few rows back and placed it above him. Ask, and you shall receive.

I settled into my seat and introduced myself to the young couple beside me for their trip home to Cookeville, Tennessee. Virginia had drawn the short straw and been seated by someone vying for the Cantankerous Man of the Year award.

I asked the young couple if they had been traveling to celebrate their anniversary because they had a sort of love-bird air about them. They told me they were just married, had actually gone on honeymoon to Italy, and they spoke of Venice and the horrible rains, how everything had been under water. And I said, "Yes, she's the eternally sinking city."

Then we were airborne, settled in for our flight. I pulled out my journal and began to write notes, trying to remember all the details of our journey and trying not to dread the picking up of the daily responsibilities of caretaking and the routine maintenance of life. In some ways it seemed easier navigating closed ferries and discovering last-minute options for trying to get to an island by midnight—to travel unknown roads with strangers, rather than to navigate the daily habits and moods of loved ones.

After we were served dinner, the couple asked me about my trip, where I'd gone and why. I tried to offer the short version. Scotland. Couchsurfing. Pilgrimage. Iona. Then they helped me get the audio working for my movie options and to make selections when it seemed my screen was broken. They had a great attitude, and I was hoping for

a good life for them. Years upon years of blissful together-
ness. They seemed like the kind of people for whom you
could see that happening.

The flight was longer than our tailwind-enabled travels
of before, but the flight attendants kept us satiated with
a constant stream of snacks, dinner, snacks, drinks, and
more snacks.

I watched the movie *Yesterday*, a rom-com spin on
an alternate reality, and *Fisherman's Friends*, an odd film
about a London music promoter who becomes friends with
a village of Cornish fishermen. Only I never saw the end of
this one, as we landed in Nashville. My seat mates declared
they'd fly with me anytime, that I was a great traveling companion, and I offered them my blessings for a happy-ever-
after life and all God's good graces.

I had determined that the easiest thing to do to retrieve
my pack was to remain on the plane until everyone else had
disembarked and I could make my way to the back where it
was stored overhead, but the woman across the aisle from
me said, "Don't worry; someone will get it for you." And
it became a group effort as the young man retrieved my
pack, and then the passengers passed it overhead, one after
the other, until it reached me rows ahead of them. It does
indeed take a village, a tribe, a community effort. The same
giving it took to live the monastic life. And the same trust
in strangers.

Someone had pointed out to me before our departure
that Mercury would be in retrograde while we traveled,

which meant you might expect delays or difficulties in travel plans and to allow for extra time in case these things occurred, but to take it all in stride and not to worry, that retrogrades could be good things as well. They made space for someone to slow their steps, to discover their strengths and find another way when needed. I had forgotten this fact as soon as it was shared with me. My cousin and I have jokes about Mercury in retrograde. My sun sign is Virgo, and she loves to read star charts and horoscopes and warn me when my ruling planet has reversed. I tell her, "Hush, I have things to do." But now I looked back and thought of the ferries and the road to Mull. Once again I considered the fact that it was the reversals, the obstacles, that revealed our strengths.

On a different trip I'd been out on the coast of Washington, on Whidbey Island, and Virginia had driven up from Oregon and picked me up so I could return with her to Portland for a few days to visit with her and her daughters. We were taking the scenic route, and along the way we saw a sign that said, "See the Largest Tree in Oregon," with an arrow that pointed through a forest. With no particular schedule or time we had to arrive, we pulled off on the side of the road and began the trek inward to see this goliath. Once we arrived, we decided it was indeed worthy of a walk and something to behold, but then we continued walking down the trail beyond the tree instead of returning to the car and picking up our drive. It was then that we saw a sign someone had made by hand, writing on a piece of wood and leaning it up against a log. It read simply, "Every Step a Prayer." Neither of us have ever forgotten that or how profound we believed it to be.

I think that sign would have been met with approval by Columba and the Celtic pagans, who had prayers for every little ordinary act.

WHEN I FIRST BEGAN my journey into deeper research and longing to set out for the Isle of Iona, I thought the Christian part of my spirituality would align just fine with whatever it was I discovered; I expected there to be a heavy influence of the pagan, the flavor decidedly ancient and earthbound. Perhaps mostly Christian with vestiges of something other than. And yet with all of that *something other than,* Iona called. And so I, unbound at last, answered.

What I found was an ancient faith that led me back again to Christ as its heartbeat and its center. I learned from all of it. It was the absolute integration of life and all things, all seasons, all beings; of the Creator and the created.

What I discovered was that the Celtic way was indeed every step a prayer. Not a prayer of need or desperation but a step and a prayer of exultation, of living, of walking out life with an awareness that all is holy.

At Iona my prayer was simple. To hold the light of Iona in my heart, to not let that light die as I returned to my daily chores and routines of living. For the divine magic of it all to stay. And then home again I went. And came. And stayed.

SOON IT WAS THANKSGIVING. I was weary from traveling so many miles. My mother agreed to a quiet little Thanksgiving. Family was all here and there this year, so we would settle for going out to eat. An act unheard-of in our Southern family. I've not been out to eat at a restaurant once for Thanksgiving in my entire life. But this year, all was simple, and I was satisfied with this.

Thanksgiving morning, I awoke and immediately felt something was wrong. My mother was eighty-seven. She might live to be one hundred, or this could be her last Thanksgiving. Eating out was okay for me but wrong for her. I went online, searched for grocery stores that might be open on Thanksgiving Day. I discovered one that was open for a few early hours, and I checked the time, got out of bed, pulled on jeans and a sweater, and said, "God, to pull this off, I don't have time to pray." Meaning, no hour of coffee with my prayer beads, no silent act of contemplation. And the answer came back swift and true: *The shopping is the prayer, and the cooking is the prayer, and the sacrifice of time is the prayer.*

So be it. It's where the rubber meets the road and the romance goes out the window. It's me waking Mom and saying, "I'm making Thanksgiving dinner; we're not going out to eat." And seeing her smile like a little girl and ask me to also get a chocolate pie. It's where all that magic-stone stuff ends up being me pushing a grocery cart, grabbing a thawed turkey and a ham and the hundred things my mother uses for her dressing, which has now fallen to me to prepare. And this could be anyone's religion. It could be the right thing to do, no matter who you are or where you're from or what God you worship. But right now, for me, this Thanksgiving, without question, it was the influence of that Celtic Christian heart that did this. Incorporating the mundane into the miracle.

I cooked Thanksgiving dinner, praying as I went. It was not my best work in the kitchen, I must confess. But still, it contained a blessing, and my mother was happy. And all was well.

27

THE PENULTIMATE PLANS OF GOD

THIS MORNING THEY HAD forecast snow to start at six a.m. Drops of rain hit the roof sporadically, then none at all. Chances of snow actually manifesting were slim to none. A promise that would melt before our eyes.

I was back on my hill, back at my writing desk, and I looked out over the little valley to the ridge beyond. I had to start early, writing before the day's duties rolled over me. But something had changed.

In all my travels with God, I had learned something new: every step was communion with the Divine. Each action we took caused an unseen reaction. I thought of all the atoms and molecules at play. Of how our very thoughts follow pathways from one synapse to another.

I love the word *synaptogenesis*, which makes the point of connectivity being crucial. Most people have heard of synapses in the brain, the connecting points between our one hundred billion brain cells. There are trillions of synapses in our brains, and these are what our brains use to connect the dots of our daily duties. Even feeding the dog has its own memorized pathway. This was either the beauty of evolution or intelligent divine design, depending on someone's point of view, and it was as amazing to me as the stars.

Returning home from pilgrimage to Iona offered me the same routines that I had left behind. Basically, nothing had changed. Not my bed, or my dog, or my mother, or her little Scottish terrier. All my routine duties awaited. All those neural pathways picked right up again. Except something was different.

Let the light of Iona live in my heart.

I could still hear the sound of my boots as I walked those empty abbey stones. Could still feel the cold through my coat and see the light of Iona filtered through the windows.

Pilgrimages are different from holidays in this way. Vacations give us a great time, a nice break from the stress of our daily lives, a phone full of photos, and a few extra pounds from the eating, maybe a tan from time in the sun. Then we return home, back to the same life, where, little by little, we settle into our same routines and work our way toward another holiday a year away.

But pilgrimage changes you. Lynne Baab wrote on her blog on spirituality: "A pilgrimage is a journey taken in search of the holy, and the Celts understood that it is impossible to encounter our Holy God without being changed in some way, perhaps as expected, or more likely, in a very unexpected way. In fact, the very nature of a pilgrimage enables us to expect the unexpected. Pilgrims give up their commitment to planning and control, and they allow God to lead and guide."

I had traveled to a holy place. It had been long and arduous. And I had been changed.

What was it in me that rose to the occasion? What was its worth? Why take the trouble to travel thousands of miles? What unseen personal transformation made it worth the while? What had I brought back with me?

I thought of the Arlington Pub with the Stone of Destiny, and the feet of the statue of Columba. Both were said to bring about some type of miracle in the making if you touched them, and I had indeed touched both.

Seven a.m. More rain came, then ice, then more rain. I waited and watched. I wanted to capture the precise moment that the rain and slush turned to the hush of huge white flakes. I wanted to witness the transformation. This molecular magic trick right before my eyes.

Rain, ice. I checked the weather again. The prediction for snow had been pushed to ten a.m. I stayed by the window. I didn't want to miss the edge of the change, the molecular manifestation of something being one thing, then another.

But then, that isn't the life we live. We drift from our twenties to our thirties and beyond, and we have become something else in the process without realizing. The miracle still exists. The change still occurred. We learn from the dark spots. We step into pools of light over and over again. Light and shadow dance through our days.

Now the rain turned to hail. Tiny pieces of ice bounced off the roof just outside the window I'd left cracked open. A deer stepped out of the woods, stood there in the front yard down the hill. Stared directly at me and held my gaze. "You too? Waiting for snow?" I said. He didn't answer or move. A young buck. Small horns. Sleek. Healthy. Beautiful. A totem animal perhaps. If so, he whispered for me to trust my instincts. To be sure and swift-footed. To be perfectly at peace and completely aware at every moment. To hold the tension between nibbling on a leaf and listening for the threat that carried death. Then came drops of rain again. The clouds couldn't decide what they were about. What message they held and would send to earth.

The road was made by walking. Yes, and perhaps we could add that sometimes it appeared that the road was made by the gravity of orbits as they slid in and out of our astrological houses with a wink and a dare. As our life unfolded before us, one shadowed minute at a time.

Whatever had made it possible for me to travel to Iona held too many factors for me to count, an equation that reached too far back to trace. But there was this. God had moved once upon a time and moves still. God had encrypted all of nature, every molecule and atom, with meaning.

From the time my faith walk started when I was a small child attending backwoods Baptist churches with my grandmother, I'd begun searching for deeper waters that I couldn't describe. A longing I couldn't put words to. Tiny arrows pointed me down the path of Celtic Christianity. It has been a journey like most of my life, filled with odd stumbles and unexpected turns. Only in looking back years later could I see that a pattern had evolved in the midst of that mess, one that revealed that my traveling to the Isle of Iona was part of my divine destination all along.

I have tried to write this story in a linear fashion. Connecting the dots as easily as the letters of the alphabet. But this story doesn't run in a straight line. It's a circle within a circle that never ends. Or, in the language of Celtic Christianity, a braid. It began before I did and will continue long after I'm gone. I am both host and guest on this journey.

I paused from communing with the deer, from writing, from watching the sky, long enough to go downstairs, give my mother her medication. Then I went to sleep.

Sometime later I woke to a blanket of white. It had happened while I wasn't watching. Transformation. Snowflakes. Tiny. Slow. Light. Love in action. A living, breathing faith. Maybe it was God telling me that it didn't matter when the miracle of transformation happened, or how long the road might be to reach our destination; it was simply about following the sound of the bells when they called and trusting that time would unfold as it should, which time has a way of doing.

O VER THE YEARS THE moment of my chasing after the Roma on the edge of the woods has haunted me, the heaviness of my stopping, turning around, my head hung down. The ordered life I returned to didn't feel like my life at all. Always, there has been this place of wounded longing for what I thought might have been. I don't think I would have made it to the wood. Someone would have eventually noticed I was missing, questioned the other children, who would have raised their little arms and simply pointed out across the fields. The military might have come searching for the missing child and found me riding a wagon, well taken care of, my feet happily dangling from the back as I watched the world roll by.

Let the light of Iona live in my heart.

The snowflakes kept falling. The hill quiet, a little wind.

The Celtic consciousness held the entire world and all creation in its heart and prayers. It was not a disparate and separate entity living on the island of a religion of its own making. Nothing was separate at all. And the ancient Celts, these ancestors of mine, were only a breath away.

The wind picked up the tiniest bit of snow from the tree branch just outside the window. It swirled and lifted, then the wind set it free again and I watched it slowly fall like the magic dust of a thousand wishes. I turned my head to listen, but no tinkling sound called. That space within me lay silent and at peace. Like that moment I had stood as if frozen in time and whispered my prayer.

Cold to the bone. Boots on stone. That peculiar light. That sense of standing in a thin place, an otherworldly place, an eternal outside-of-time place. As if all the Celtic people and Irish monks and nuns stood alongside me. And we were right there, all alive together.

Let the light of Iona live in my heart.

"DID YOU FIND WHAT you were looking for? Was it what you hoped for? What you had expected?"

People asked me these questions when I returned. The truth was, I had hoped for nothing. Had expected nothing. It was simple. Iona had called to me. Had been calling for a long time. Since I was a child. And in the fullness of time, in due season, I had answered.

If you talk to people about Iona, they will all tell you one thing. They will say this with a type of reverence about this birthplace of Celtic Christianity. Just two simple words.

The light.

Spiritual Practices Inspired By Celtic Christianity

W HEN I FIRST HEARD the words *Celtic Christianity* and began to study the subject, I found that some of the disciplines and qualities it incorporates came very naturally to me. Which led me to believe that applying these principles to my everyday life would be a snap. I was wrong.

Playing piano came very naturally to me. I could sound out parts of "Born Free" when I was in third grade, never having taken a lesson. When my mother discovered I had this natural talent, she enrolled me in piano lessons. She actually bought a piano, put it in the living room, and each week I walked to lessons from my house. I was a fine student—right up until the day I quit. Refused to practice or go again. I've always faulted my mother for letting me get away with this because it was easier than looking back and recognizing my own self-discipline issues, or perhaps acknowledging that that code phrase, *attention deficit*, might have had something to do with it. Or maybe it was simply because *Gilligan's Island* came on at the same time as those lessons. No matter the reason—sadly, my piano playing ended there. I can still pick out a few notes of "Born Free." That's about it.

Much like my yoga practice, which does my body and mind better than any physical exercise I've discovered, the Celtic practices needed to go beyond reading about and gaining knowledge of them. I needed to actually apply the principles of Celtic Christianity to my daily life.

First, I realized, I would need a plan. At least a set of practices that I reviewed each week to see if I had employed those great things and observe how they were affecting my life for the better. In this way I could discover what areas of my life might be lacking most, and record which practices made a difference as I incorporated them into a regular weekly routine. The following are practices that I've begun. Some weeks I'm better at reaching my goals than others; that's part of being human. And the Celtic attitude I've discovered is to rely on those parts of me that are infused with God's goodness and light, and to let that (rather than guilt) be my great guide.

I've listed these practices below with a short description of each and some notes about their application. This is not an all-inclusive list of Celtic Christian practices. It is my list of recommendations based on what has worked for me. I hope you'll find them as beneficial and strengthening as I have.

In Peace and Light,

—River

Pilgrimage

Let's begin with the act of going on a pilgrimage because this is a tough one, I think, for most people. And I greatly appreciate your going on pilgrimage with me to Iona through reading *The Ancient Way*. I hope the story connected with you in such a way that you felt like you were right there with me.

The act of going on pilgrimage is embraced by many religions, and by different denominations of Christianity. The act of pilgrimage requires the sacrifice of time and leaving the sacred space of one's home and life to venture to a place that is considered holy. Maybe it is just a place that calls to you, like Machu Picchu or the Grand Canyon does to many people. Places of pilgrimage don't have to be "Christian," per se. For one person it may be a World Heritage site, and for another it may be one of the natural wonders of the world, where travelers from around the world feel inspired, or we might say called, to visit. People from all walks of life and all religions have shared with me spiritual experiences they've had at these places.

The Celtic people were wanderers. They moved frequently and trusted that God was with them on the journey and would be waiting for them wherever they arrived. Now there are tour companies and groups that offer special "Celtic Pilgrimages" to sites that are famous because of the Celtic Christians. What I would recommend is this:

If you desire to incorporate going on a pilgrimage into your life, allow yourself time to pray, reflect, and meditate on where you feel called to go. One thing Celtic Christianity is *not* is something that hurries and worries you. As in, "I must go on pilgrimage this month to have a transformation to better myself or become who I want to be!" You have all the time you need. I know you might say, "Well, River, that's not what you wrote about *you* doing." Yes, I know. But I was also concerned about finishing my book. Most people are not trying to incorporate a pilgrimage into a book deadline. And in that respect, you can take five years mulling over the pilgrimage idea before you actually do it.

I will point out, however, that your desire to go to see some small village in Italy and drink great wine in a vineyard or perhaps to see the Eiffel Tower at night while you sip Champagne might not qualify as great pilgrimage material. You get the idea. Nor does it need to be in the jungles of the Congo where you have to swim through leeches to make it count. Pilgrimage is not punishment. Is it sometimes difficult to reach? Yes. Here's what I know. I trust you. Truly, I do. I trust you to get a sense of what place might be calling to you, where God might be leading you, and the time that is right for you to make your plans to undertake a pilgrimage. Remember, it doesn't have to be a place that is so far away you must fly over the ocean and ride a camel up a mountain. The place of your pilgrimage might be the Blue Ridge Mountains or somewhere in your region of the world. The focus is to purpose in your heart and mind that you are going on a pilgrimage to edify your spirit, to learn something from God or about yourself, to pay honor to something or someone or God.

Prayer

The Celtic people were known to say prayers over just about everything. There was a prayer for lighting the fire, a prayer for protection, a prayer for this and a prayer for that. Prayers that led the way through the days and into the night.

I know a little something about prayer in that I'm just an ordinary girl who has tried to incorporate prayer in different ways throughout my life. I know the prayers of a child, the prayers my grandmother said over meals, the prayers I said over my sons when they were little, and the ones I prayed when they were deployed. I know the prayers I've said for strangers and the ones I've said for family and friends. And after all these years and all those prayers, I still feel I've just touched the tip of the iceberg.

Prayer is not just a never-ending petition of desires and intercessions for ourselves and others. Prayer is communication, and this is something those ancient Celts and early Christians got right. They got down to the basics of prayer so that it was threaded through their lives in ways that I haven't managed to do. They didn't have to have a set prayer time or go to church to pray because they prayed as they went. Their lives were a prayer. One of the greatest points made in all my research about Columba and his monks is that Celtic Christianity was very much about the priests and monks saying, "Do as I do." Not "Do as I say." They made it a point to live their lives so that people could look at them and see exactly what they believed. They really were living epistles. For them, perfection was never the goal.

What I've tried to do while embracing Celtic Christianity is offer one story of what these practices look like. I've used my prayer beads to pray as a matter of starting my day and focusing myself into prayer. If I didn't do this, I would grab my phone and scroll through social media feeds. I also have a habit of carrying my prayer beads with me, either in my purse or in a pocket, because when I come across them, they remind me to live in prayer. If I'm driving and stuck in traffic and there are my prayer beads, I remember this precisely. That maybe I can pray for others stuck in traffic, or for our safety getting home, or for anything or anyone that comes to mind. And I keep bringing myself back to prayer being a kind of communion, a conversation, and in that, I realize sometimes I need to just be quiet and listen. Which brings us to the next practice.

Contemplation, Stillness, and Silence

I link these three together because contemplation requires the other two. The Celtic Christian tradition came from Ireland, and the priests there were greatly influenced by the desert fathers and mothers of early Christianity and their sense of aloneness with God—what it represented and how it was of benefit. They were contemplatives who were often sequestered or became hermits. That's not what God is calling most of us to do, although some days we swear we'd be better off alone in a cave for a good six months. Finding both the time and space to actually be silent and still, and to contemplate long enough to remember the passwords to our email accounts, is challenge enough. Being able to do this long enough to gain spiritual peace and perspective seems downright impossible. Which is exactly the reason that it is one of the disciplines we need most. I've searched for ways to incorporate this into my daily life. I've found a few that work—and a bevy of ways that don't.

Whether it is due to the challenges of my life or my personal habits, I find that rising earlier than anyone around me is pretty much a prerequisite if I'm to find this kind of time daily. Only in the silence before the world wakes up can I achieve a singular kind of stillness that leads to contemplation. The Episcopal cathedral in Nashville has contemplative services a few times a week. I don't go as often as I would like, but every time I do, these services—though simple and short—benefit me greatly. Many churches now offer contemplative services on Sundays or another day of the week. I recommend that you find one in your community and give it a try. It may be something you enjoy so much you incorporate it into your weekly routine.

Another thing I find extremely beneficial is to go on a silent (or mostly silent) retreat. If I could do so for even forty-eight hours once a month, I would. Many retreat centers, monasteries, and houses of prayer are open around the nation. They take reservations and often require only a love offering for your stay. This is one of the greatest ways I find I can incorporate a time for serious contemplation and silence into my life. It has been one of the most fruitful of spiritual disciplines for me. Not all retreats are completely silent, but many have longer stretches of silence, with the opportunity to also meet once with a spiritual director during your stay. While I've gone for extended periods, I've found three days is ideal, as it takes at least a full day for me to process the noise in my brain, slow my mind down, and get to a place where I can actually be still, and silent, and contemplative.

Celebrating Creation

It surprises me how often I can drive up the long path to my house, get out of the car, and go straight inside with my mind a busy bag of to-do lists and concerns and not even notice the beauty of all creation around me. I'm surrounded by trees and wildlife, in some seasons flowers, in all seasons a view across to the ridge beyond me. And yet I can be blind to the beauty.

The Celtic people were excellent at recognizing the Creator in the beauty of creation. It was truly a part of their nature, this sense that the Divine is at our fingertips, before our eyes, and beneath our feet. They didn't just believe God created these things; they believed God was actually *in* the creation. I've always been someone who lives close to the earth, in the way I was brought up. My parents and grand-parents came from very rural parts of North Florida, what we called the back woods, and being outside a lot as a child, being free to roam through the woods and creeks with my cousins, was a wonderful part of my childhood. I contin-ued to appreciate these things as I grew up on the beach, swam in the Gulf, canoed with my friends, even at night as the stars came out. It would be difficult for me to see these things and be in touch with them and not believe in some great divine creator. But I began to appreciate them to a greater degree when I started delving into Celtic Christian-ity. They took on added significance. My level of apprecia-tion went way up when I contemplated all of creation—the rocks, oceans, woods—possessing what I might call divine properties. Now this was no longer a tree; it was a sacred, *alive* thing, and something that I wanted to joyfully cele-brate. It's brought me to a place of new appreciation of just being in nature; taking a walk becomes a type of prayer.

I encourage you to incorporate a way to enjoy nature. We don't all have to go whitewater-rafting or hike in the mountains to be one with the outdoors. Find a favorite path to walk or a place where you just love to sit and meditate on being in nature. That can be just the thing that fuels your divine connection and creativity.

Hospitality

In *The Ancient Way* I've written a great deal about hospitality. It truly was one of the characteristics of the Celtic people and the way that they shared their lives with others. It's one of the greatest ways to honor the Divine, as we embrace the wonderful opportunity to connect with other people, to effectively welcome them to our home and our hearth, however we choose to do that. Obviously, Couchsurfing turned out to be an amazing way for me to meet people and make new friends by accepting their hospitality.

Only you know what is right for you. But I encourage you to look for areas in your life where you feel you could either offer hospitality to someone or accept someone else's gift of hospitality. Traveling or inviting someone into your home may not be something you can do right now for whatever reason, but there are other ways to be hospitable. I can offer my hospitality to people who need assistance, such as people who are homebound and the elderly, serving at a homeless shelter, hosting a church event. When we determine in our hearts to incorporate something into our lives, the Divine has a way of opening the door to those opportunities.

The Art of Imagination

This is something that struck me as a writer and artist: the Celtic people created some of the most beautifully crafted works of pen, of stone, of paint, of wood. Their intricate work in metals and design is spectacular. Such artworks as *The Book of Kells* and other works, and the popularity of reproductions of their designs, showcase how these people, so connected to the earth, painstakingly created beautiful works of art and, in so doing, celebrated the gifts of a creative God.

If your life is like mine, in that it takes a little work to enjoy creating new things, drawing, painting, exploring that creative side of your nature, you might set aside a little time each week to explore artistic endeavors that interest you. As you do so, think of the great gift of imagination and how this gift comes from an imaginative God. We mirror the Divine, and when we explore these artistic passions, we are celebrating that part of the Divine within us.

Time

One of the things that I sensed the most during my visit to Iona was something about time that I have been hard pressed to communicate. And it may be one of those things that I never find the words for. But this sense of time illuminated the fact that somehow, we all stand together throughout time. Those who came before us singing God's praises, saying blessings as they broke bread or held the hand of a neighbor in need, are somehow connected to us. Somehow we are all right here together. The Celtic people were attuned to time, to the threshold of day becoming night and night becoming day again. In studying about them, I discovered no sense of rush or hurry, but rather a focus on the time they were in, a focus on the act of living in the moment. It's popular now to practice living in the moment. But it was something they didn't have to practice; they simply did it.

You might ask yourself, "How do I view time? Does it seem too hurried to me? Or do I feel I never have enough hours in the day to do what I need to do?" I have learned of late to become aware of time from a different perspective. To see it as inhabited by the presence of the Creator. As I do so, it is as though time shapes itself to hold all that I need, if I will simply walk through it in prayerful awareness of the magnificence of the moment. Of fully possessing it. This is a practice. It is not something I achieve with regularity, but it is a practice that, when I attend to it, enriches my life immeasurably.

Anam Cara

The Ancient Way speaks of the Celtic understanding of friendship described by John O'Donohue as *anam cara*. Celtic histories stress the importance of this type of friendship. Life holds enough challenges that you need someone to both accompany you and guide you. While our lives don't allow for every person to be an intimate friend who knows our ups and downs, strengths and weaknesses, life does offer us the opportunity to make such a friend and be such a friend. If you don't have someone you feel you can completely trust with your true self, being absolutely transparent, then consider how you might pursue a deeper friendship with someone you know, or find a place to meet new people and develop such a friendship. And it's a spiritual practice to also be this kind of friend: a true, nonjudgmental, knowing, and wise friend for someone else. If you have such a mentor-friend in your life, now is a great time to write or call that person to let them know you care. If not, it's never too late to become someone's *anam cara* in this world.

Community

I'm not a big one for embracing community. I blame it on being an introvert. And that's fair. But one of the things I love most about the Celtic people was their commitment to community, to a shared way of working together for the common good. This was true of Columba and his monks, of the nuns at the monastery so many years ago on Iona.

Through belonging to a book event that has been running for over twenty years and brings more than three hundred women together annually, I have come to appreciate community in a greater way than ever before. And church and other communities that involve gathering regularly have helped me understand how people go from being acquaintances to knowing one another as a group. To care when someone falls ill or to grieve when someone dies. To celebrate the marriages and births and achievements of each member. And to be stronger together than we are individually. This is a Celtic practice I've come to understand, even as I still have room for growth.

I've begun to make a point of meeting some of my neighbors. Funny how you can live on a street or in a neighborhood and not even associate with those closest to you. My growing understanding of Celtic Christians has me determined to be more like them. Through just a little bit of patience and a bit of effort to widen the circle of community, my world has been enriched.

ACKNOWLEDGMENTS

As no endeavor ever comes to fruition without being borne on the wings of others, I'd like to take a moment to say thank you.

To Lil Copan, thank you for recognizing the spark that was this story and allowing it to follow its own path across Scotland and home again.

To Alison Vandenberg, director of marketing; Emily Benz, marketing manager; Annette Hughes, national sales director; and the entire team at Broadleaf Books for giving birth to *The Ancient Way* with such creative enthusiasm. My special appreciation to two special people who edited *The Ancient Way* with precision and passion—Rachel Reyes and Heidi Mann. You both mastered the magic of making me look better than I am.

To the people of the UK for putting up with me in my travels, pointing me in the right direction, getting me on and off the "tube," the taxi, the train—all with a kind word or smile. You remind me that we are not strangers.

To the people of Scotland, you wild storytelling tribe! Oh, how I love you and long to return.

To the beautiful Gail of Edinburgh who, without knowing me at all, offered open arms and doors. Kitchen tables. True Scottish porridge, full moons, and the goodness of a goddess.

To James of Glasgow for your great patience in late nights and wild ferry rides and that Oban 14 Scotch that's as smooth as warm silk. And for driving me all the way to Iona and back again. And for graciously sending me your beautiful words of the names of places along our route I didn't write down.

To Malcolm and Maggie Guite, for your wealth of charm and hospitality in a world away and for the surprise of discovering Columba in your kitchen.

To Wendy Grisham, for keeping me well and warm in your village and giving me a chance to discover my words again anew an ocean away.

To the secret angels who made the journey possible. You know who you are. Your wings, these words.

To Brent Bill, for always being a calm and positive voice of faith and for introducing me to Lil Copan.

To Ami McConnell and Wes Yoder, for your powerful encouragement and work on this project.

To my friend, Virginia Dixon, for trekking to Scotland with me. Who knew way back in our Bay High School days such an adventure awaited?

To J. Philip Newel and (the late) John O'Donohue, for opening my heart to the spiritual sensibilities of Celtic Christianity.

And to the readers everywhere who discover these words and find that the light of Iona calls to you. Godspeed you on your good journey.

NOTES

Chapter 5

The quote about Bible translation as both science and art is from the introduction to the Holman Christian Standard Bible (Nashville: Holman Bible Publishers, 2003)—the Bible with the Celtic design on the cover that the author's mother bought and subsequently gifted to her.

"I bind unto myself today . . ." is a prayer attributed to St. Patrick, from the time of his ministry in Ireland during the fifth century. Various adaptations have been made.

Chapter 9

The quote from Julian of Norwich (1342–1416) is from her *Revelation of Love*. A version edited by John Skinner was published by Doubleday (New York) in 1997. See pp. 54–55, 124.

Chapter 11

John O'Donohue's phrase "Celtic consciousness being a penumbral light" is from his book *Anam Cara: A Book of Celtic Wisdom* (1998; repr., New York: Harper Perennial), p. 80.

Chapter 21

The story and quote from Robert Macfarlane are found on pages 144–145 of *The Old Ways: A Journey on Foot* (New York: Penguin Books, 2013).

Chapter 24

The Kindlings is "an international, relational movement dedicated to rekindling the spiritual, creative, intellectual legacy of Christians in culture," according to founder Dick Staub's website: https://dickstaub.com/about/the-kindlings/.

Malcolm Guite's grandmother's book: Janette I. W. Murray, *A Legendary of St. Mungo* (Glasgow and London: Gowans & Gracy, 1923).

Chapter 27

The quote from Lynne Baab can be found here: "Celtic Christianity: Pilgrimage and the Celtic Sense of Place," *Lynne Baab* (blog), April 22, 2015, https://tinyurl.com/yx647tzt. The website is subtitled "Resources for Personal Spirituality and for Congregational Leaders."

For Further Reading

Extravagant Love: Reflections of a Catholic Yogi, Craig Bullock
Short Trip to the Edge: Where Heaven Meets Earth–
    A Pilgrimage, Scott Cairns
The Celtic Way of Prayer, Esther De Waal
To Hear the Forest Sing, Margaret Dulaney
Thin Places Everywhere, Bruce Epperly
Holy Rover, Lori Erickson
A Little History of the World, E. H. Gombrich
The Singing Bowl, Malcolm Guite
Walking on Water: Reflections on Faith and Art, Madeleine
    L'Engle
The Business of Heaven, C. S. Lewis
Searching for Stars on an Island in Maine, Alan Lightman
The Unspoken Sermons, George MacDonald
The Old Ways: A Journey on Foot, Robert Macfarlane

The Cosmic Mystery Tour: A High-Speed Journey through Space and Time, Nicholas Mee

New Seeds of Contemplation, Thomas Merton

An Iona Prayer Book, Peter Millar

The Book of Creation, J. Philip Newell

Celtic Benediction: Morning and Night Prayer, J. Philip Newell

Celtic Prayers from Iona, J. Philip Newell

A Prayer Journal, Flannery O'Connor

Anam Cara: A Book of Celtic Wisdom, John O'Donohue

Walking in Wonder: Eternal Wisdom for a Modern World, John O'Donohue

Illuminating the Way: Embracing the Wisdom of Monks and Mystics, Christine Valters Paintner

The Soul's Slow Ripening: 12 Celtic Practices for Seeking the Sacred, Christine Valters Paintner

Late Migrations, Margaret Renkl

The Order of Time, Carlo Rovelli

Celtic Christianity, Ray Simpson

Christian Wisdom of the Jedi Masters, Dick Staub

The Lessons of St. Francis, John Michael Talbot

Mystics of the Church, Evelyn Underhill

Love and Quasars: An Astrophysicist Reconciles Faith and Science, Paul Wallace

The Treasury of Christian Spiritual Classics, Thomas Nelson Publishers